Allyn & Bacon
Casebook Series
Community Practice

Edited by

Jerry L. Johnson

Grand Valley State University

George Grant, Jr.

Grand Valley State University

Boston   New York   San Francisco
Mexico City   Montreal   Toronto   London   Madrid   Munich   Paris
Hong Kong   Singapore   Tokyo   Cape Town   Sydney

To all of those who have helped, advised, supported, criticized,
and forgiven. You know who you are.
Jerry L. Johnson

To my wife, Beverly, who inspires and supports me
in all my endeavors. In loving memory of my father and mother,
George and Dorothy Grant, and Daisy Franks.
George Grant, Jr.

Series Editor: *Patricia Quinlin*
Marketing Manager: *Kris Ellis-Levy*
Production Administrator: *Janet Domingo*
Compositor: *Galley Graphics*
Composition Buyer: *Linda Cox*
Manufacturing Buyer: *JoAnne Sweeney*
Cover Coordinator: *Rebecca Krzyzaniak*

For related titles and support materials, visit our online catalog at www.ablongman.com.

Library of Congress Cataloging-in-Publication Data

Allyn & Bacon casebook series for community practice / edited by Jerry L. Johnson,
    George Grant, Jr.—1st ed.
      p. cm.
    Includes bibliographical references.
    ISBN 0-205-38955-4 (pbk.)
      1. Community-based social services—Case studies.   2. Community development—Case
    studies.   3. Community organization—Case studies.   I. Title: Allyn and Bacon casebook
    series for community practice.   II. Title: Casebook series for community practice.   III.
    Johnson, Jerry L.   IV. Grant, George, Jr.
    HV41. A432 2004

                                                                                        2004056836

Printed in the United States of America

10   9   8   7   6   5   4   3   2   1   09   08   07   06   05   04

Contents

Preface

This text offers students the chance to study the work of experienced social workers performing community practice in the U.S. and around the world. As graduate and undergraduate social work educators, we (the editors) have struggled to find quality practice materials that translate well into a classroom setting. Over the years, we have used case materials from our practice careers, professionally produced audio-visuals, and tried other casebooks. While each had its advantages, we could not find a vehicle that allowed students to study the work of experienced practitioners that took students beyond the belief that practice is a technical endeavor that involves finding "correct" interventions to solve client problems.

We want our students to study and analyze how experienced practitioners think about practice and how they struggle to resolve ethical dilemmas and make treatment decisions that meet the needs of their clientele. We want students to review and challenge the work of others in a way that allows them to understand what comprises important practice decisions with real clients in real practice settings. That is, we want classroom materials that allow students entry into the minds of experienced practitioners.

Goals of the Casebook

This Casebook focuses on practice with clients in community-based settings and from diverse backgrounds. Our goal is to provide students with an experience that:

1. Provides personal and intimate glimpses into the thinking and actions of experienced practitioners as they work with clients. In each case, students may

demonstrate their understanding of the cases and how and/or why the authors approached their case in the manner presented.

2. Provides a vehicle to evaluate the process, ideas, and methods used by the authors. We also wanted to provide students a chance to present their ideas about how they would have worked differently with the same case.

3. Affords students the opportunity to use evidence-based practice findings (Gibbs, 2003; Cournoyer, 2004) as part of the case review and planning process. We challenge students to base practice judgments and case planning exercises on current practice evidence available through library and/or electronic searches, and practice wisdom gained through consultation and personal experience when the evidence is conflicted or lacking.

To meet our goals, the cases we included in this text focus on the practice *process,* specifically client engagement, assessment, and the resultant clinical process, including the inevitable ethical dilemmas that consistently arise in daily practice. We aim to demonstrate the technical and artistic elements involved in developing and managing the various simultaneous processes involved in practice. While we recognize the difficulty of presenting process information (circular) in a linear medium (book), we have tried to do the best job possible toward this end.

To achieve our goals, we include four in-depth case studies in this text. In these case studies, authors guide students through the complete practice process, from initial contact to client termination and practice evaluation. Focusing heavily on multi-systemic client life history (see Chapter 1), students get a detailed look into the life history and presentation of clients. Then, we challenge students by using client information and classroom learning to develop a written narrative assessment, diagnostic statement, treatment and intervention plan, termination and follow-up plan, and a plan to evaluate practice. We have used these cases as in-class exercises, the basis for semester-long term papers, and as comprehensive final examinations that integrate multifaceted student learning in practice courses across the curriculum.

Rationale

As former practitioners, we chose the cases carefully. Therefore, the cases in this text focus on the process (thinking, planning, and decision-making) of social work practice and not necessarily on techniques or outcome. Do not be fooled by this statement. Obviously, we believe in successful client outcome based, at least in part, on the use of evidence-based practice methods and current research findings. As important as this is, it is not our focus here—with good reason. Our experience suggests that instructive process occurs in cases that have successful and unsuccessful outcome. In fact, we often learned more from unsuccessful cases than successful cases. We learned the most when events did not play out as planned. While some of the cases terminated successfully, others did not. This is not a commentary on the author or the author's skill level. Everyone has cases (sometimes too many) that do not turn out as planned. We chose cases based on one simple criterion: did it provide the best possible hope for practice education? We asked authors to teach practice by considering cases that were interesting and difficult, regardless of outcome. We did not want the Casebook to become simply a vehicle to promote practice brilliance.

Mostly, we wanted this text to differ from other casebooks, because we were unsatisfied with casebooks as teaching tools. As part of the process of planning our Casebooks, we reviewed other casebooks and discussed with our graduate and undergraduate students approaches that best facilitated learning in the classroom. We discovered that many students were also dissatisfied with a casebook approach to education, for a variety of reasons. Below, we briefly address what our students told us about casebooks in general.

1. *Linear presentation.* One of the most significant problems involves case presentation. Generally, this involves two issues: linearity and brevity. Most written case studies give students the impression that practice actually proceeds smoothly, orderly, and in a sequential manner. These cases often leave students believing—or expecting—that clinical decisions are made beforehand and that practice normally proceeds as planned. In other words, students often enter the field believing that casework follows an "*A, leads to B, leads to C, leads to clients living happily ever after*" approach.

Experienced practitioners know better. In over 40 years of combined social work practice in a variety of settings, we have learned—often the "hard way"—that the opposite is true. We rarely, if ever, had a case proceed sequentially, whether our client is an individual, couple, family, group, community, or classroom. That is, the process of engagement (including cultural competence), assessment, treatment planning, intervention, and follow-up occur in a circular manner, rooted in the client's social, physical, and cultural context, and includes consideration of the practitioner, his or her organization, and the laws and policies that affect and/or determine the boundaries of social work practice and treatment funding.

Practice evolves in discontinuous cycles over time, including time-limited treatments mandated by the managed care system. Therefore, real-life clinical practice—just as in all developing human relationships—seems to consistently require stops and starts, take wrong turns, and even, in some cases, require "do-overs." While the goal of competent practice is to facilitate an orderly helping process that includes planned change (Timberlake, Farber, & Sabatino, 2002), practice, as an orderly process, is more often a goal (or a myth) than planned certainty. Given the linearity of case presentations discussed above, readers are often left without an appreciation or understanding of practice as process.

Additionally, many of the case presentation texts we reviewed provided "hard" client data and asked students to develop treatment plans based on this data. Yet, as any experienced practitioner knows, the difficulty in practice occurs during engagement and data collection. The usual case approach often overlooks this important element of practice. While a book format limits process writing, we believe that the case format we devised here brings students closer to the "real thing."

2. *Little focus on client engagement.*   As we like to remind students, there are two words in the title of our profession: social and work. In order for the "work" to be successful, students must learn to master the "social"—primarily client engagement and relationship building. Social work practice is relationship based (Saleebey, 2002) and, from our perspective, relies more on the processes involved in relationship building and client engagement than technical intervention skills (Johnson, 2004). Successful practice is often rooted more in the ability of practitioners to develop open and trusting relationships with client(s) than on their ability to employ specific methods of intervention (Johnson, 2004).

Yet, this critically important element of practice often goes understated or ignored. Some texts even assume that engagement skills somehow exist before learning about practice. We find this true in casebooks and primary practice texts as well. When it is discussed, engagement and relationship building is presented as a technical process that also proceeds in linear fashion. Our experience with students, employees, and practitioner/trainees over the last two decades suggests that it is wrong to assume that students and/or practitioners have competent engagement or relationship building skills. From our perspective, developing a professional relationship that involves trust and openness, where clients feel safe to dialogue about the most intimate and sometimes embarrassing events in their lives, is the primary responsibility of the practitioner, and often spells the difference between positive and negative client outcome (Johnson, 2004; Miller & Rollnick, 2002; Harper & Lantz, 1996). Hence, each case presentation tries to provide a sense of this difficult and often elusive process and some of the ways that the authors overcame challenges to the culturally competent client engagement process.

Target Audience

Our target audience for this text, and the others in the series, are advanced undergraduate as well as foundation and advanced graduate students in social work and other helping disciplines. We have tested our approach with students at several different points in their education. We find that the casebooks can be used as:

- An adjunct learning tool for undergraduates preparing for or already involved in their field practicum.
- Practice education and training for foundation-level graduate students in practice theory and/or methods courses.
- An adjunct learning tool for second-year graduate students in field practicum.
- An adjunct learning tool for undergraduate and/or graduate students in any practice courses pertaining to specific populations.

While we are social work educators, we believe the casebooks will be useful in social work and other disciplines in the human services, including counseling psychology, counseling, mental health, psychology, and specialty disciplines such as marriage and family therapy, substance abuse, and mental health degree or certificate programs. Any educational or training program designed to prepare students to work with clients in a helping capacity may find the casebooks useful as a learning tool.

Structure of Cases

We organized the case studies to maximize critical thinking, the use of professional literature, evidenced-based practice knowledge, and classroom discussion in the learning process. At various points throughout each case, we comment on issues and/or dilemmas highlighted by the case. Our comments always end with a series of questions designed to focus student learning by calling on their ability to find and evaluate evidence from the professional literature and through classroom discussion. We ask students to collect evidence on different sides of an issue, evaluate that evidence, and develop a professional position that they can defend in writing and/or discussion with other students in the classroom or seminar setting.

We hope that you find the cases and our format as instructive and helpful in your courses as we have in ours. We have field-tested our format in courses at our university, finding that students respond well to the length, depth, and rigor of the case presentations. Universally, students report that the case materials were an important part of their overall learning process.

Organization of the Text

We organized this text to maximize its utility in any course. Chapter 1 provides an overview of the Advanced Multi-Systemic (AMS) practice approach. We provide this as one potential organizing tool for students to use while reading and evaluating the subsequent cases. This chapter offers students an organized and systematic framework to use when analyzing cases and/or formulating narrative assessments, treatment, and intervention plans. Our intent is to provide a helpful tool, not make a political statement about the efficacy or popularity of one practice framework versus others. In fact, we invite faculty and students to apply whatever practice framework they wish when working the cases.

In Chapter 2, *Kristi J. Gleeson, MSW* presents her community development work in the Republic of Albania in a chapter entitled **Golem, Albania.** After many years living under repressive Communism, follow the progress of a small group of concerned citizens in Golem, a rural Albanian village, as they press local authorities for potable water. Gleeson explains the problems and pitfalls of working in formerly Communist countries, and the need to understand culture and history.

In Chapter 3, *Kimberly S. Crawford, BS* and *Jerry L. Johnson, Ph.D.* present an interesting case entitled **Mothers vs. The Board of Education,** demonstrating that a group of mothers in a community can, indeed, "take on city hall." In this case about a local neighborhood issue, Crawford and Johnson present an unusual case that shows what can happen when a group of formerly disempowered women find empowerment in the face of overwhelming resistance and odds.

In Chapter 4, *Jerry L. Johnson, Ph.D.* presents the first part of a case entitled **Organizing Social Work in the Republic of Armenia: Part I.** In Part I, Johnson discusses the background of a need assessment and organizing project he performed in the Republic of Armenia. The U.S. government and World Bank wanted him to determine whether it was possible to create and fund a comprehensive training program for social workers in Armenia. Chapter 4 provides the information needed to intervene in this case.

The final chapter, **Organizing Social Work in the Republic of Armenia: Part II,** presents the completion of the case begun in Chapter 4. In this chapter, Johnson presents the final data and report provided to authorities in Armenia. He also discusses the outcome of this project 18 months after its completion.

Acknowledgments

We would like to thank the contributors to this text, Kristi J. Gleeson and Kimberly S. Crawford, for their willingness to allow their work to be challenged and discussed in a public venue. We would also like to thank Patricia Quinlin and her people at Allyn and Bacon for their faith in the Casebook Series and in our ability to manage fourteen manuscripts at once. Additionally, we have to thank all of our students and student assistants that served as "guinea pigs" for our case studies. Their willingness to provide honest feedback contributes mightily to this series.

Jerry L. Johnson—I want to thank my wife, Cheryl, for her support and willingness to give me the time and encouragement to write and edit. I also owe a debt of gratitude to my dear friend Hope, for being there when I need you the most.

George Grant, Jr.— I want to thank Dean Rodney Mulder, Dr. Elaine Schott, Dr. Doris Perry, and Professor Emily Jean McFadden for their insight, encouragement, and support during this process. Finally, I want to thank Alice D. Denton and Alyson D. Grant for their continued support and Dr. Julius Franks and Professor Daniel Groce for their intellectual discourse and unwavering support.

Contributors

The Editors

Jerry L. Johnson, Ph.D., MSW is an Associate Professor in the School of Social Work at Grand Valley State University in Grand Rapids, Michigan. He received his MSW from Grand Valley State University and his Ph.D. in sociology from Western Michigan University. Johnson has been in social work for more than 20 years as a practitioner, supervisor, administrator, consultant, teacher, and trainer. He was the recipient of two Fulbright Scholarship awards to Albania in 1998–99 and 2000–01. In addition to teaching and writing, Johnson serves in various consulting capacities in countries such as Albania and Armenia. He is the author of two previous books, *Crossing Borders—Confronting History: Intercultural Adjustment in a Post-Cold War World* (2000, Rowan and Littlefield) and *Fundamentals of Substance Abuse Practice* (2004, Wadsworth Brooks/Cole).

George Grant, Jr., Ph.D., MSW is an Associate Professor in the School of Social Work at Grand Valley State University in Grand Rapids, Michigan. Grant, Jr., also serves as the Director of Grand Valley State University's MSW Program. He received his MSW from Grand Valley State University and Ph.D. in sociology from Western Michigan University. Grant, Jr., has a long and distinguished career as practitioner, administrator, consultant, teacher, and trainer in social work, primarily in fields dedicated to Child Welfare.

Contributors

Kristi J. Gleason, MSW received her MSW degree in 2000 from Grand Valley State University in Grand Rapids, Michigan. Gleeson also won a Fulbright Award in 2000–01. She has since spent two years in Tirana, Albania, teaching, researching domestic violence and women's issues, and working for an NGO on community development in the capital city and surrounding villages. Currently, she works in the People's Republic of China on a Child Rights program for migrant children and children with disabilities.

Kimberly S. Crawford, BS received her bachelor's degree in psychology from Grand Valley State University in Grand Rapids, Michigan. She is also an MSW degree candidate at Grand Valley State University. Over the years, Crawford has become involved in numerous grassroots campaigns and has significant experience in the community advocating for social justice.

Bibliography

Cournoyer, B. R. (2004). *The evidence-based social work skills book.* Boston: Allyn and Bacon.

Gibbs, L. E. (2003). *Evidence-based practice for the helping professions: A practical guide with integrated multimedia.* Pacific Grove, CA: Brooks/Cole.

Harper, K. V., & Lantz, J. (1996). *Cross-cultural practice: Social work practice with diverse populations.* Chicago: Lyceum Books.

Johnson, J. L. (2004). *Fundamentals of substance abuse practice.* Pacific Grove, CA: Brooks/Cole.

Miller, W. R., & Rollnick, S. (2002). *Motivational interviewing: Preparing people to change addictive behavior* (2nd ed.). New York: Guilford Press.

Saleebey, D. (2002). *The strengths perspective in social work practice* (3rd ed.). Boston: Allyn and Bacon.

Timberlake, E. M., Farber, M. Z., & Sabatino, C. A. (2002). *The general method of social work practice: McMahon's generalist perspective* (4th ed.). Boston: Allyn and Bacon.

1

A Multi-Systemic Approach to Practice

Jerry L. Johnson & George Grant, Jr.

This is a practice-oriented text, designed to build practice skills with individuals, families, and groups. We intend to provide you the opportunity to study the process involved in treating real cases from the caseloads of experienced practitioners. Unlike other casebooks, we include fewer cases, but provide substantially more detail in hopes of providing a realistic look into the thinking, planning, and approach of the practitioners/authors. We challenge you to study the authors' thinking and methods to understand their approach and then use critical thinking skills and the knowledge you have gained in your education and practice to propose alternative ways of treating the same clients. In other words, what would your course of action be if you were the primary practitioner responsible for these cases? Our hope is that this text provides a worthwhile and rigorous experience studying real cases as they progressed in practice.

Before proceeding to the cases, we include this chapter as an introduction to the Advanced Multi-Systemic (AMS) practice perspective. We decided to present this introduction with two primary goals in mind. First, we want you to use the information contained in this chapter to help assess and analyze the cases in this text. You will have the opportunity to complete a multi-systemic assessment, diagnoses, treatment, and intervention plan for each case. This chapter will provide the theoretical and practical basis for this exercise. Second, we hope you find that AMS makes conceptualizing cases clearer in your practice environment. We do not suggest that AMS is the only way, or even the best way for every practitioner to conceptualize cases. We simply know, through experience, that AMS is an effective way to think about practice with client-systems of all sizes and configurations. While there are many approaches to practice, AMS offers an effective way to place clinical decisions in the context of client lives and experiences, making engagement and treatment productive for clients and practitioners.

Advanced Multi-Systemic (AMS) Practice

Sociological Roots

> Whether the point of interest is a great power state or a minor literary mood, a family, a prison, and a creed—these are the kinds of questions the best social analysts have asked. They are the intellectual pivots of classic studies of (person) in society—and they are the questions inevitably raised by any mind possessing the sociological imagination. For that imagination is the capacity to shift from one perspective to another—from the political to the psychological; from examination of a single family to comparative assessment of the national budgets of the world; from the theological school to the military establishment; from considerations of an oil industry to studies of contemporary poetry. It is the capacity to range from the most impersonal and remote transformations to the most intimate features of the human self—and see the relations between the two. Back of its use is always the urge to know the social and historical meaning of the individual in the society and in the period in which he (or she) has his quality and his (or her) being. (Mills, 1959, p. 7; parentheses added)

Above, sociologist C. Wright Mills provided a seminal description of the sociological imagination. As it turns out, Mills's sociological imagination is also an apt description of AMS. Mills believed that linking people's "private troubles" to "public issues" (p. 2) was the most effective way to understand people and their issues, by placing them in historical context. It forces investigators to contextualize individuals, families, and communities in the framework of the larger social, political, economic, and historical environments in which they live. Ironically, this is also the goal of social work practice (Germain & Gitterman, 1996; Longres, 2000). Going further, Mills (1959) stated:

> We have come to know that every individual lives, from one generation to the next, in some society; that he (or she) lives out a biography, and that he (or she) lives it out within some historical sequence. By the fact of his (or her) living he (or she) contributes, however minutely, to the shaping of this society and to the course of its history, even as he (or she) is made by society and by its historical push and shove. (p. 6)

Again, Mills was not speaking as a social worker. He was an influential sociologist, speaking about a method of social research. In *The Sociological Imagination,* Mills (1959) proposed this as a method to understand the links between people, their daily lives, and their multi-systemic environment. Yet, while laying the theoretical groundwork for social research, Mills also provided the theoretical foundation for an effective approach to social work practice. We find four relevant points in *The Sociological Imagination* that translate directly to social work practice.

1. It is crucial to recognize the relationships between people's personal issues and strengths (private troubles) and the issues (political, economic, social, historical, and legal) and strengths of the multi-systemic environment (public issues) in which people live daily and across their life span. A multi-systemic understanding includes recognizing and integrating issues and strengths at the micro (individual, family, extended kin, etc.), mezzo (local community), and macro (state, region, national, and international policy, laws, political, economic, and social) levels during client engagement, assessment, treatment, follow-up, and evaluation of practice. This is true whether your client is an individual, family, small group, or community association. This requirement does not change, only the point where investigation begins.

2. This depth of understanding (by social workers and, especially, clients) can lead to change in people's lives. We speak here about second-order change, or, significant change that makes a long-term difference in people's lives; change that helps people view themselves differently in relationship to their world. This level of change becomes possible when people, alone or in groups, make multi-systemic links in a way that makes sense to them (Freire, 1993). In other words, clients become "empowered" to change when they understand their life in the context of their world and realize that they have previously unforeseen or unimagined choices in how they live, think, believe, and act.

3. Any assessment and/or clinical diagnoses that exclude multi-systemic links do not provide a holistic picture of people's lives, their troubles, and/or strengths. In sociology, this leads to a reductionist view of people and society, while in social work it reduces the likelihood that services will be provided (or received by clients) in a way that addresses client problems and utilizes client strengths in a meaningful way. The opportunity for change is reduced whenever client life history is overlooked because it does not fit, or is not called for, in a practitioner's preferred method of helping, or because of shortcuts many people believe are needed in a managed care environment. One cannot learn too much about their clients, their lives, and their attitudes, beliefs, and values as it relates to the private troubles presented in treatment.

4. Inherent in AMS and foundational to achieving all that was discussed above relies on practitioners being able to rapidly develop rapport with clients and client systems that leads to engagement in treatment or action. In this text, client engagement

> . . . occurs when you develop, in collaboration with clients, a trusting and open professional relationship that promotes hope and presents viable prospects for change. Successful engagement occurs when you create a social context in which vulnerable

people (who often hold jaded attitudes toward helping professionals) can share their innermost feelings, as well as their most embarrassing and shameful behavior with you, a *total stranger.* (Johnson, 2004, p. 93; emphasis in original)

AMS Overview

First, we should define two important terms that comprise AMS. Understanding these terms is important, because they provide the foundation for understanding the language and concepts used throughout the remainder of this chapter.

1. Advanced.   According to Derezotes (2000), "the most advanced theory is also the most inclusive" (p. viii). AMS is advanced because it is inclusive. It requires responsible practitioners, in positions of responsibility (perhaps as solo practitioners), to acquire a depth of knowledge, skills, and self-awareness that allows for an inclusive application of knowledge acquired in the areas of human behavior in the social environment, social welfare policy, social research and practice evaluation, and multiple practice methods and approaches in service of clients and client systems of various sizes, types, and configurations.

AMS practitioners are expected to have the most inclusive preparation possible, "both the broad generalist base of knowledge, skills, and values and an in-depth proficiency in practice . . . with selected social work methods and populations" (Derezotes, 2000, p. xii). Hence, advanced practitioners are well trained and, with in-depth knowledge, are often in positions of being responsible for clients as primary practitioners. They are afforded the responsibility for engaging, assessing, intervening, and evaluating practice, ensuring that clients are ethically treated in a way that is culturally competent and respectful of their client's worldview. In other words, AMS practitioners develop the knowledge, skills, and values needed to be leaders in their organizations, communities, the social work profession, and especially in the treatment of their clients. The remainder of this chapter explains why AMS is an advanced approach to practice.

2. Multi-systemic.   From the earliest moments in their education, social workers learn a systems perspective that emphasizes the connectedness between people and their problems to the complex interrelationships that exist in their client's world (Timberlake, Farber, & Sabatino, 2002). To explain these connections, systems theory emphasizes three important concepts: wholeness, relationships, and homeostasis. Wholeness refers to the notion that the various parts or elements (subsystem) of a system interact to form a whole that best describes the system in question. This concept asserts that no system can be understood or explained unless the connectedness of the subsystems to the whole are understood or explained. In other words, the whole is greater than the sum of its parts. Moreover, systems theory also posits that change in one subsystem will affect change in the system as a whole.

In terms of systems theory, relationship refers to the patterns of interaction and overall structures that exist within and between subsystems. The nature of these relationships is more important than the system itself. That is, when trying to understand or explain a system (individual, family, or organization, etc.) how subsystems connect through relationships, the characteristics of the relationships between subsystems, and how the subsystems interact provide clues to understanding the system as a whole. Hence, the application of systems theory is primarily based on understanding relationships. As someone once said about systems theory, in systems problems occur between people and subsystems (relationships), not "in" them. People's internal problems relate to the nature of the relationships in the systems where they live and interact.

Homeostasis refers to the notion that most living systems work to maintain and preserve the existing system, or the status quo. For example, family members often assume roles that serve to protect and maintain family stability, often at the expense of "needed" change. The same can be said for organizations, groups, or community associations. The natural tendency toward homeostasis in systems represents what we call the "dilemma of change" (Johnson, 2004). This can best be described as the apparent conflict, or what appears to be client resistance or lack of motivation, that often occurs when clients approach moments of significant change. Systems of all types and configurations struggle with the dilemma of change: should they change to the unknown or remain the same, even if the status quo is unhealthy or unproductive? Put differently, systems strive for stability, even at the expense of health and well-being of individual members and/or the system itself.

What do we mean, then, by the term *multi-systemic*? Clients (individuals, families, communities, etc.) are systems that interact with a number of different systems simultaneously. These systems exist and interact at multiple levels, ranging from the micro level (individual and families), the mezzo level (local community, institutions, organizations, the practitioner and their agency, etc.), to the macro level (culture, laws and policy, politics, oppression and discrimination, international events, etc.). How these various systems come together, interact, and adapt, along with the relationships that exist within and between each system work together to comprise the "whole" that is the client, or client-system.

In practice, the client (individual, couple, family, community, etc.) is not the "system," but one of many interacting subsystems in a maze of other subsystems constantly interacting to create the system—the client plus elements from multiple subsystems at each level. It would be a mistake to view the client as the whole system. They are but one facet of a multidimensional and multi-level system comprised of the client and various other subsystems at the micro, mezzo, and macro levels.

Therefore, the term *multi-systemic* refers to the nature of a system comprised of the various multi-level subsystems described above. A multi-systemic perspective recognizes that clients or client systems are *one part or subsystem* in relationship with other subsystemic influences occurring on different levels. This level of understanding—the system as the whole produced through multi-systemic subsystem interactions—is the main unit of investigation for practice. As stated above, it is narrow to consider the client as a functioning independent system with peripheral involvement with other systems existing outside of their intimate world. These issues and relationships work together to help shape and mold the client who, in turn, shapes and molds his or her relationship to the other subsystems. Yet, the person-of-the-client is but one part of the system in question during practice.

AMS provides an organized framework for gathering, conceptualizing, and analyzing multi-systemic client data and for proceeding with the helping process. It defines the difference between social work and other disciplines in the helping professions at the level of theory and practice. How, you ask? Unlike other professional disciplines that tend to focus on one or a few domains (i.e., psychology, medicine, etc.), AMS provides a comprehensive and holistic "picture" of clients or client-systems in the context of their environment by considering information about multiple personal and systemic domains simultaneously. Moreover, practitioners can use AMS to address clients and client systems of all sizes and configurations. That is, this approach works as well with communities or international projects as it does with individuals or families seeking therapy.

Resting on the generalist foundation taught in all Council on Social Work Education (CSWE) accredited undergraduate and foundation-level graduate programs, AMS requires practitioners to contextualize client issues in the context of the multiple interactions that occur between the client/client-system and the social, economic, legal, political, and physical environment in which the client lives. It is a unifying perspective based in the client's life, history, and culture that guides the process of collecting and analyzing client life information and intervening to promote personal choice through a comprehensive, multi-systemic framework. Beginning with culturally competent client engagement, a comprehensive multi-systemic assessment points toward a holistically based treatment plan that requires practitioners to select and utilize appropriate practice theories, models, and methods—or combinations thereof—that best fit the client's unique circumstances and needs.

AMS is not a practice theory, model, or method itself. It is a perspective or framework for conceptualizing client-systems. It relies on the practitioner's ability to use a variety of theories, models, and methods, and to incorporate knowledge from human behavior, social policy, research/evaluation, and practice into his or her routine approach with clients. For example, an AMS practitioner will have the skills to apply different approaches to individual treatment (client-centered, cognitive-behavioral, etc.), family treatment (structural, narrative, Bowenian, etc.), work with couples, in groups, arrange for specialized care if needed, and as an advocate on behalf of their client. It may also require practitioners to treat clients in a multi-modal approach (i.e., individual and group treatments simultaneously). Additionally, AMS practitioners can work with community groups and organizations at the local, regional, or national level.

Practitioners not only must know how to apply different approaches but also how to determine, primarily through the early engagement and assessment process, which theory, model, or approach (direct or indirect, for example) would work best for a particular client. Hence, successful practice using AMS relies heavily on the practitioner's ability to competently engage and multi-systemically assess client problems and strengths. Practitioners must simultaneously develop a sense of their client's personal interaction and relationship style—especially related to how they relate to authority figures—when determining which approach would best suit the client. For example, a reserved, quiet, or thoughtful client or someone who lacks assertiveness may not be well served by a directive, confrontational approach, regardless of the practitioner's preference. Moreover, AMS practitioners rely on professional practice research and outcome studies to help determine which approach or intervention package might work best for particular clients and/or client-systems. AMS expects practitioners to know how to find and evaluate practice research in their practice areas or specialties.

Elements of the Advanced Multi-Systemic Approach to Social Work Practice

The advanced multi-systemic approach entails the following seven distinct, yet integrated elements of theory and practice. Each is explained below.

Ecological Systems Perspective

One important subcategory of systems therapy for social work is the ecological systems perspective. This perspective combines important concepts from the science of ecology and general systems theory into a way of viewing client problems and strengths in social work practice. In recent years, it has become the prevailing perspective for social work practice (Miley, O'Melia, & DuBois, 2004). The ecological systems perspective—sometimes referred to as the ecosystems perspective—is a useful metaphor for guiding social workers as they think about cases (Germain & Gitterman, 1980).

Ecology focuses on how subsystems work together and adapt. In ecology, adaptation is "a dynamic process between people and their environments as people grow, achieve competence, and make contributions to others" (Greif, 1986, p. 225). Insight from ecology leads to an analysis of how people fit within their environment and what adaptations are made in the fit between people and their environments. Problems develop as a function of inadequate or improper adaptation or fit between people and their environments.

General systems theory focuses on how human systems interact. It focuses specifically on how people grow, survive, change, and achieve stability or instability in the complex world of multiple systemic interactions (Miley, O'Melia, & DuBois, 2004). General systems theory has contributed significantly to the growth of the family therapy field and to how social workers understand their clients.

Together, ecology and general systems theory evolved into what social workers know as the ecological systems perspective. The ecological systems perspective provides a systemic framework for understanding the many ways that persons and environments interact. Accordingly, individuals and their individual circumstances can be understood in the context of these interactions. The ecological systems perspective provides an important part of the foundation for AMS. Miley, O'Melia, and DuBois (2004) provide an excellent summary of the ecological systems perspective. They suggest that it

1. Presents a dynamic view of human beings as system interactions in context.
2. Emphasizes the significance of human system interactions.
3. Traces how human behavior and interaction develop over time in response to internal and external forces.
4. Describes current behavior as an adaptive fit of "persons in situations."
5. Conceptualizes all interaction as adaptive or logical in context.
6. Reveals multiple options for change within persons, their social groups, and in their social and physical environments (p. 33).

Social Constructionism

To maintain AMS as an inclusive practice approach, we need to build on the ecological systems perspective by including ideas derived from social constructionism. Social constructionism builds on the ecological systems perspective by introducing ideas about how people define themselves and their environment. Social constructionism also, by definition, introduces the role of culture in the meaning people give to themselves and other systems in their multi-systemic environments. The ecological systems perspective discusses relationships at the systemic level. Social constructionism introduces meaning and value into the equation, allowing for a deeper understanding and appreciation of the nature of multi-systemic relationships and adaptations.

Usually, people assume that reality is something "out there" that hits them in the face, something that independently exists, and people must learn to "deal with it." Social constructionism posits something different. Evolving as a critique of the "one reality" belief system, social constructionism points out that the world is comprised of multiple realities. People define their own reality and then live within those definitions. Accordingly, the definition of reality will be different for everyone. Hence, social constructionism deals primarily with meaning, or the systemic processes by which people come to define themselves in their social world. As sociologist W. I. Thomas said, in what has become known as the Thomas Theorem, "If people define situations as real, they are real in their consequences."

For example, some people believe that they can influence the way computerized slot machines pay out winnings by the way they sit, the feeling they get from the machine as they look at it in the casino, by the clothes they are wearing, or by how they trigger the machine, either by pushing the button or pulling the handle. Likewise, many athletes believe that a particular article of clothing, a routine for getting dressed, and/or a certain pregame meal dictates the quality of their athletic prowess that day.

Illogical to most people, the belief that they can influence a computerized machine, that the machine emits feelings, or that an article of clothing dictates athletic prowess is real to some people. For these people, their beliefs influence the way they live. Perhaps you have ideas or "superstitutions" that you believe influence how your life goes on a particular day. This is a common occurrence. These people are not necessarily out of touch with objective reality. While people may know, at some level, that slot machines pay according to preset, computerized odds or that athletic prowess has nothing to do with dressing routines, the belief systems continue. What dictates the behavior and beliefs discussed above or in daily "superstitutions" have nothing to do with objective reality and everything to do with people's subjective reality. Subjective reality—or a person's learned definition of the situation—overrides objectivity and helps determine how people behave and/or what they believe.

While these examples may be simplistic, according to social constructionism, the same processes influence everyone—always. In practice, understanding that people's behavior does not depend on the objective existence of something, but on their subjective interpretation of it, is crucial to effective application of AMS. This knowledge is most helpful during client engagement. If practitioners remember that practice is about understanding people's perceptions and not objective reality, they reduce the likelihood that clients will feel misunderstood, there will be fewer disagreements, and it becomes easier to avoid the trap of defining normal behavior as client resistance or a diagnosable mental disorder. This perspective contributes to a professional relationship based in the client's life and belief systems, is consistent with his or her worldview, and one that is culturally appropriate for the client. Being mindful that the definitions people learn from their culture underlies not only what they do but also what they perceive, feel, and think places practitioners on the correct path to "start where the client is." Social constructionism emphasizes the cultural uniqueness of each client and/or client-system and the need to understand each client and/or client-system in his or her own context and belief systems, not the practitioner's context or belief systems.

Social constructionism also posits that different people attribute different meaning to the same events, because the interactional contexts and the way individuals interpret these contexts are different for everyone, even within the same family or community. One cannot assume that people raised in the same family will define their social world similarly. Individuals, in the context of their environments, derive meaning through a complex process of individual interpretation. This is how siblings from the same family can be so different, almost as if they did not grow up in the same family. For example, the sound of gunfire in the middle of the night may be frightening or normal, depending upon where a person resides and what is routine and accepted in his specific environment. Moreover, simply because some members of a family or community understand nightly gunfire as normal does not mean that others in the same family or community will feel the same.

Additionally, social constructionism examines how people construct meaning with language and established or evolving cultural beliefs. For example, alcohol consumption is defined as problematic depending upon how the concept of "alcohol problem" is socially constructed in specific environments. Clients from so-called drinking cultures may define drinking six alcoholic drinks daily as normal, while someone from a different cultural background may see this level of consumption as problematic. One of the authors worked in Russia and found an issue that demonstrates this point explicitly. Colleagues in Russia stated rather emphatically that consuming one "bottle" (approximately a U.S. pint) of vodka per day was acceptable and normal. People that consume more than one bottle per day were defined as having a drinking problem. The same level of consumption in the United States would be considered by most as clear evidence of problem drinking.

Biopsychosocial Perspective

Alone, the ecological systems perspective, even with the addition of social constructionism, does not provide the basis for the holistic understanding required by AMS. While it provides a multi-systemic lens, the ecological systems perspective focuses mostly on externals. That is, how people interact and adapt to their environments and how environments interact and adapt to people. Yet, much of what practitioners consider "clinical" focuses on "internals" or human psychological and emotional functioning. Therefore, the ecological systems perspective provides only one part of the holistic picture required by the advanced multi-systemic approach. By adding the biopsychosocial perspective, practitioners can consider the internal workings of human beings to help explain how external and internal subsystems interact.

What is the biopsychosocial perspective? It is a theoretical perspective that considers how human biological, psychological, and social-functioning subsystems interact to account for how people live in their environment. Similar to social systems, human beings are also multidimensional systems comprised of multiple subsystems constantly interacting in their environment, the human body. The biopsychosocial perspective applies multi-systemic thinking to individual human beings.

Several elements comprise the biopsychosocial perspective. Longres (2000) identifies two dimensions of individual functioning, the biophysical, and the psychological; subdividing the psychological into three subdimensions: the cognitive, affective, and behavioral. Elsewhere, we added the spiritual/existential dimension to this conception (Johnson, 2004). Understanding how the biological, psychological, spiritual and existential, and social subsystems interact is instrumental in developing an appreciation of how individuals influence and are influenced by their social systemic environments. Realizing that each of these dimensions interacts with external social and environmental systems allow practitioners to enlarge their frame of reference, leading to a more holistic multi-systemic view of clients and client-systems.

Strengths/Empowerment Perspective

Over the last few years, the strengths perspective has emerged as an important part of social work theory and practice. The strengths perspective represents a significant change in how social workers conceptualize clients and client-systems. According to Saleebey (2002), it is "a versatile practice approach, relying heavily on ingenuity and creativity . . . Rather than focusing on problems, your eye turns toward possibility" (p. 1). Strengths-based practitioners believe in the power of possibility and hope in helping people overcome problems by focusing on, locating, and supporting existing personal or systemic strengths and resiliencies. The strengths perspective is based on the belief that people, regardless of the severity of their problems, have the capabilities and resources to play an active role in helping solve their own problems. The practitioner's role is to engage clients in a way that unleashes these capabilities and resources toward solving problems and changing lives.

Empowerment

Any discussion of strengths-based approaches must also consider empowerment as an instrumental element of the approach. Empowerment, as a term in social work, has evolved over the years. We choose a definition of empowerment that focuses on power; internal, interpersonal, and environmental (Parsons, Gutierrez, & Cox, 1998). According to Parsons, Gutierrez, and Cox (1998),

> In its most positive sense, power is (1) the ability to influence the course of one's life, (2) an expression of self worth, (3) the capacity to work with others to control aspects of public life, and (4) access to the mechanisms of public decision making. When used negatively, though, it can also block opportunities for stigmatized groups, exclude others and their concerns from decision-making, and be a way to control others. (p. 8)

Hence, empowerment in practice is a process (Parsons, Gutierrez, and Cox, 1998) firmly grounded in ecological systems and strength-based approaches that focus on gaining power by individuals, families, groups, organizations, or communities. It is based on two related assumptions: (1) all human beings are potentially competent, even in extremely challenging situations, and (2) all human beings are subject to various degrees of powerlessness (Cox & Parsons, 1994, p. 17) and oppression (Freire, 1993). People internalize their sense of powerlessness and oppression in a way that their definition of self in the world is limited, often eliminating any notion that they can act in their own behalf in a positive manner.

An empowerment approach makes practical connections between power and powerlessness. It illuminates how these factors interact to influence clients in their daily life. Empowerment is not achieved through a single intervention, nor is it something that can be "done" to another. Empowerment does not occur through neglect or by simply giving responsibility for life and well-being to the poor or troubled, allowing them to be "free" from government regulation, support, or professional assistance. In other words, empowerment of disenfranchised groups does not occur simply by dismantling systems (such as the welfare system) to allow these groups or individuals to take responsibility for themselves. Hence, empowerment does not preclude helping.

Consistent with our definition, empowerment develops through the approach taken toward helping, not the act of helping itself. Empowerment is a sense of gained or regained power that someone attains in his or her life that provides the foundation for change in the short term, and stimulates belief in his or her ability to positively influence life over the long term. Empowerment occurs as a function of the long-term approach of the practitioner and the professional relationship developed between practitioner and client. One cannot provide an empowering context through a constant focus on problems, deficits, inadequacies, negative labeling, and dependency.

The Power of Choice

Choice is an instrumental part of strengths-based and empowerment approaches, by recognizing that people, because of inherent strengths and capabilities, can make informed choices about their lives, just like people who are not clients. Practitioners work toward offering people choices about how they define their lives and problems, the extent to which they want to address their problems, and the means or mechanisms through which change should occur. Clients become active and instrumental partners in the helping process. They are not passive vessels, waiting for practitioners to "change them" through some crafty intervention or technique.

We are not talking about the false choices sometimes given to clients by practitioners. For example, clients with substance abuse problems are often told that they must either abstain or leave treatment. Most practitioners ignore or use as evidence of denial, client requests to attempt so-called controlled use. If practitioners were interested in offering true choice, they would work with these clients toward their controlled-drinking goal in an effort to reduce the potential harm that may result from their use of substances (Johnson, 2004; van Wormer & Davis, 2003), even if the practitioner believes that controlled drinking is not possible. Abstinence would become the goal only when their clients choose to include it as a goal.

Client Engagement as Cultural Competence

Empowerment (choice) occurs through a process of culturally competent client engagement, created by identifying strengths, generating dialogue targeted at revealing the extent of people's oppression (Freire, 1993), and respecting their right to make informed choices in their lives. Accordingly, empowerment is the "transformation from individual and collective powerlessness to personal, political, and cultural power" (GlenMaye, 1998, p. 29), through a strengths-based relationship with a professional helper.

Successful application of AMS requires the ability to engage clients in open and trusting professional relationships. The skills needed to engage clients from different backgrounds and with different personal and cultural histories are what drives practice; what determines the difference between successful and unsuccessful practice. Advanced client engagement skills allow the practitioner to elicit in-depth, multi-systemic information in a dialogue between client and practitioner (Johnson, 2004), providing the foundation for strengths-based client empowerment leading to change.

Earlier, we defined client engagement as a mutual process occurring between clients and practitioners in a professional context, created by practitioners. In other words, creating the professional space and open atmosphere that allows engagement to flourish is the primary responsibility of the practitioner, not the client. Practitioners must have the skills and knowledge to adjust their approach toward specific clients and the client's cultural context and not *vice versa*. Clients do not adjust to us and our beliefs, values, and practices—we adjust to them. When that occurs, the foundation exists for client engagement. By definition, relationships of this nature must be performed in a culturally competent manner. Yet, what does this mean?

Over the last two decades, social work and other helping professions have been concerned with cultural competence in practice (Fong, 2001). Beginning in the late 1970s, the professional literature has been replete with ideas, definitions, and practice models designed to increase cultural awareness and promote culturally appropriate practice methods. Yet, despite the attention given to the issue, there remains confusion about how to define and teach culturally competent practice.

Structural and Historical Systems of Oppression: Who Holds the Power?

Often embedded in laws, policies, and social institutions are oppressive influences such as racism, sexism, homophobia, and classism, to name a few. These structural issues play a significant role in the lives of clients (through maltreatment and discrimination) and in social work practice. How people are treated (or how they internalize historical treatment of self, family, friends, and/or ancestors) shapes how they believe, think, and act in the present. Oppression affects how they perceive that others feel about them, how they view the world and their place in it, and how receptive they are to professional service providers. Therefore, culturally competent practice must consider the impact of structural systems of oppression and injustice on clients, their problems, strengths, and potential for change.

Oppression is a by-product of socially constructed notions of power, privilege, control, and hierarchies of difference. As stated above, it is created and maintained by differences in power. By definition, those who have power can force people to abide by the rules, standards, and actions the powerful deem worthwhile, mandatory, or acceptable. Those who hold power can enforce particular worldviews; deny equal access and opportunity to housing, employment, or health care; define right and wrong, normal and abnormal; and imprison, confine, and/or commit physical, emotional, or mental violence against the powerless (McLaren, 1995; Freire, 1993). Most importantly, power permits the holder to "set the very terms of power" (Appleby, 2001, p. 37). It defines the interaction between the oppressed and the oppressor, and between the social worker and client.

Social institutions and practices are developed and maintained by the dominant culture to meet *its* needs and maintain *its* power. Everything and everybody is judged and classified accordingly. Even when the majority culture develops programs or engages in helping activities, these efforts will not include measures that threaten the dominant group's position at the top of the social hierarchy (Freire, 1993). For example, Kozol (1991) wrote eloquently about how public schools fail by design, while Freire (1993) wrote about how state welfare and private charity provide short-term assistance while ensuring that there are not enough resources to lift people permanently out of poverty.

Oppression is neither an academic nor a theoretical consideration; it is not a faded relic of a bygone era. Racism did not end with the civil rights movement, and sexism was not eradicated by the feminist movement. Understanding how systems of oppression work in people's lives is of paramount importance for every individual and family seeking professional help, including those who belong to the *same* race, gender, and class as the practitioner. No two individuals, regardless of their personal demographics, experience the world in the same way. Often, clients are treated ineffectively by professional helpers who mistakenly believe that people who look or act the same will experience the world in similar ways. These workers base their assumptions about clients on stereotypic descriptions of culture, lifestyle, beliefs, and practices. They take group-level data (i.e., many African American adolescents join gangs because of broken families and poverty) and assume that *all* African American teenagers are gang members from single-parent families. Social work values and ethics demand a higher standard, one that compels us to go beyond stereotypes. Our job is to discover, understand, and utilize personal differences in the assessment and treatment process to benefit clients, not use differences as a way of limiting clients' potential for health and well-being.

We cannot accurately assess or treat people without considering the effects of oppression related to race, ethnicity, culture, sexual preference, gender, or physical/emotional status. We need to understand how oppression influences our clients' beliefs about problems and potential approaches to problem solving, and how it determines what kind of support they can expect to receive if they decide to seek help. For example, despite the widely held belief that chemical dependency is an equal opportunity disease (Gordon, 1993), it is clear that some people are more vulnerable than others. While some of the general themes of chemical dependency may appear universal, each client is unique. That is, an individual's dependency results from personal behavior, culture (including the history of one's culture), past experiences, and family interacting with larger social systems that provide opportunities or impose limits on the individual (Johnson, 2000).

Systems of oppression ensure unequal access to resources for certain individuals, families, and communities. However, while all oppressed people are similar in that they lack the power to define their place in the social hierarchy, oppression based on race, gender, sexual orientation, class, and other social factors is expressed in a variety of ways. Learning about cultural nuances is important in client assessment, treatment planning, and treatment (Lum, 1999). According to Pinderhughes (1989), there is no such thing as culture-free service delivery. Cultural differences between clients and social workers in terms of values, norms, beliefs, attitudes, lifestyles, and life opportunities affect every aspect of practice.

What Is Culture?

Many different concepts of culture are used in social work, sociology, and anthropology. Smelser (1992) considers culture a "system of patterned values, meanings, and beliefs that give cognitive structure to the world, provide a basis for coordinating and controlling human interactions, and constitute a link as the system is transmitted from one generation to another" (p. 11). Geertz (1973) regarded culture as simultaneously a product of and a guide to people searching for organized categories and interpretations that provide a meaningful experiential link to their social life. Building upon these two ideas, in this book we abide by the following definition of culture proposed elsewhere (Johnson, 2000):

> Culture is historical, bound up in traditions and practices passed through generations; memories of events—real or imagined—that define a people and their worldview. (Culture) is viewed as collective subjectivity, or a way of life adopted by a community that ultimately defines their worldview. (p. 121)

Consistent with this definition, the collective subjectivities called culture are pervasive forces in the way people interact, believe, think, feel, and act in their social world. Culture plays a significant role in shaping how people view the world. As a historical force, in part built on ideas, definitions, and events passed through generations, culture also defines people's level of social acceptance by the wider community; shapes how people live, think, and act; and influences how people perceive that others feel about them and how they view the world and their place in it. Thus, it is impossible to understand a client without grasping his or her cultural foundations.

Cultural Competence

As stated earlier, over the years many different ideas and definitions of what constitutes culturally competent practice have developed, as indicated by the growth of the professional literature since the late 1970s. To date, focus has primarily been placed in two areas: (1) the need for practitioners to be aware or their own cultural beliefs, ideas, and identities leading to cultural sensitivity, and (2) learning factual and descriptive information about various ethnic and racial groups based mostly on group-level survey data and analyses. Fong (2001) suggests that culture is often considered "tangential" to individual functioning and not central to the client's functioning (p. 5).

To address this issue, Fong (2001) builds on Lum's (1999) culturally competent practice model that focuses on four areas: (1) cultural awareness, (2) knowledge acquisition, (3) skill development, and (4) inductive learning. Besides inductive learning, Lum's model places focuses mainly on practitioners in perpetual self-awareness, gaining knowledge about cultures, and skill building. While these are important ideas for cultural competence, Fong (2001) calls for a shift in thinking and practice, "to provide a culturally competent service focused solely on the client rather than the social worker and what he or she brings to the awareness of ethnicity" (p. 5). Fong (2001) suggests an "extension" (p. 6) of Lum's model by turning the focus of each of the four elements away from the practitioner toward the client. For example, cultural awareness changes from a practitioner focus to "the social worker's understanding and the identification of the critical cultural values important to the client system and to themselves" (p. 6). This change allows Fong (2001) to remain consistent with the stated definition of culturally competent practice, insisting that practitioners,

> . . . operating from an empowerment, strengths, and ecological framework, provide services, conduct assessments, and implement interventions that are reflective of the clients' cultural values and norms, congruent with their natural help-seeking behaviors, and inclusive of existing indigenous solutions. (p. 1)

While we agree with the idea that "to be culturally competent is to know the cultural values of the client-system and to use them in planning and implementing services" (Fong, 2001, p. 6), we want to make this shift the main point of a culturally competent model of client engagement. That is, beyond what should or must occur, we believe that professional education and training must focus on the skills of culturally competent client engagement that are necessary to make this happen; a model that places individual client cultural information at the center of practice. We agree with Fong (2001) that having culturally sensitive or culturally aware practitioners is not nearly enough. Practitioner self-awareness and knowledge of different cultures does not constitute cultural competence. We strive to find a method for reaching this worthy goal.

The central issue revolves around practitioners participating in inductive learning and the skills of grounded theory. In other words, regardless of practitioner beliefs, awarenesses, or sensitivities, their job is to learn about and understand their client's world, and "ground" their theory of practice in the cultural context of their client. They develop a unique theory of human behavior in a multi-systemic context for every client. Culturally competent client engagement does not happen by assessing the extent to which client lives "fit" within existing theory and knowledge about reality, most of which is middle-class and Eurocentric at its core. Cultural competence (Johnson, 2004)

> . . . *begins* with learning about different cultures, races, personal circumstances, and structural mechanisms of oppression. It *occurs* when practitioners master the interpersonal skills needed to move beyond general descriptions of a specific culture or race to learn specific individual, family, group, or community interpretations of culture, ethnicity, and race. The culturally competent practitioner knows that within each culture are individually interpreted and practiced thoughts, beliefs, and behaviors that may or may not be consistent with group-level information. That is, there is tremendous diversity within groups, as well as between them. Individuals are unique unto themselves,

not simply interchangeable members of a specific culture, ethnicity, or race who naturally abide by the group-level norms often taught on graduate and undergraduate courses on human diversity. (p. 105)

Culturally competent client engagement revolves around the practitioner's ability to create a relationship, through the professional use of self, based in true dialogue (Freire, 1993; Johnson, 2004). We define dialogue as "a joint endeavor, developed between people (in this case, practitioner and client) that move clients from their current state of hopelessness to a more hopeful, motivated position in their world" (Johnson, 2004, p. 97). Elsewhere (Johnson, 2004), we detailed a model of culturally competent engagement based on Freire's (1993) definitions of oppression, communication, dialogue, practitioner self-work, and the ability to exhibit worldview respect, hope, humility, trust, and empathy.

To investigate culture in a competent manner is to take a comprehensive look into people's worldviews—to discover what they believe about the world and their place in it. It goes beyond race and ethnicity (although these are important issues) into how culture determines thoughts, feelings, and behaviors in daily life. This includes what culture says about people's problems; culturally appropriate strengths and resources; the impact of gender on these issues; and what it means to seek professional help (Leigh, 1998).

The larger questions to be answered are how clients uniquely and individually interpret their culture; how their beliefs, attitudes, and behaviors are shaped by that interpretation, and how these cultural beliefs and practices affect daily life and determine lifestyle in the context of the larger community. Additionally, based on their cultural membership, beliefs, and practices, practitioners need to discover the potential and real barriers faced by clients in the world. Many clients, because they are part of non-majority cultures, face issues generated by social systems of oppression such as racism, sexism, homophobia, and ethnocentrism that expose them to limitations and barriers that others do not face.

What is the value of culturally competent client engagement? Helping clients discuss their attitudes, beliefs, and behaviors in the context of their culture—including their religious or spiritual belief systems—offers valuable information about their worldview, sense of social and spiritual connection, and/or practical involvement in their social world. Moreover, establishing connections between their unique interpretation of their culture and their daily life provides vital clues about people's belief systems, attitudes, expectations (social construction of reality), and explanation of behaviors that cannot be understood outside the context of their socially constructed interpretation of culture.

A Cautionary Note

It is easy to remember to ask about culture when clients are obviously different (i.e., different races, countries of origin, etc.). However, many practitioners forgo cultural investigation with clients they consider to have the same cultural background as the practitioner. For example, the search for differences between European

Americans with Christian beliefs—if the social worker shares these characteristics—gets lost in mutual assumptions, based on the misguided belief that there are no important differences between them. The same is often true when clients and practitioners come from the same racial, cultural, or lifestyle backgrounds (i.e., African American practitioner and client, gay practitioner and gay client, etc.). Culturally competent practice means that practitioners are always interested in people's individual interpretation of their culture and their subjective definitions of reality, whether potential differences are readily apparent or not. Practitioners must be diligent to explore culture with clients who appear to be from the same background as the practitioner, just as they would with people who are obviously from different cultural, racial, ethnic, or religious backgrounds.

Multiple Theories and Methods

No single theory, model, or method is best suited to meet the needs of all clients (Miley, O'Melia, & DuBois, 2004). Consistent with this statement, one of the hallmarks of AMS is the expectation that practitioners must determine which theory, model, or method will best suit a particular client. Choosing from a range of approaches and interventions, AMS practitioners develop the skills and abilities to: (1) determine, based on the client's life, history, culture, and style, which treatment approach (theory and/or method) would best suit their needs and achieve the desired outcome, (2) determine which modality or modalities (individual, family, group treatment, etc.) will best meet the need of their clients, and (3) conduct treatment according to their informed clinical decisions.

Over the last 20 years or so, graduate social work education has trended toward practice specialization through concentration-based curricula. Many graduate schools of social work build on the generalist foundation by insisting that students focus on learning specific practice models or theories (disease, cognitive-behavioral, psychoanalysis, etc.) and/or specific practice methods (individual, family, group, etc.), often at the exclusion of other methods or models. For example, students often enter the field intent on doing therapy with individuals, say, from a cognitive-behavioral approach only.

This trend encourages practitioners to believe that one approach or theory best represents the "Truth." Truth, in this sense, is the belief that one theory or approach works best for most people, most of the time. It helps create a practice scenario that leads practitioners to use their chosen approach with every client they treat. Therefore, practice becomes a process of the practitioner forcing clients to adjust to the practitioner's beliefs and expectations about the nature of problems, the course of treatment, and definition of positive versus negative outcomes. From this perspective, what is best for clients is determined by what the practitioner believes is best, not what clients believe is in their best interest.

Some practitioners take their belief in the Truth of a particular theory or method to extremes. They believe that one model or theory works best for all people, all the time. We found this to be common in the family therapy field, whereby some true believers insist that everyone needs family therapy—so that is all they offer. What's worse is that many of these same practitioners know and use only one particular family therapy theory and model. The "true believer" approach can cause problems, especially for clients. For example, when clients do not respond to treatment, instead of looking to other approaches, true believers simply prescribe more of the method that did not work in the first place. If a more intensive application of the method does not work, then the client's "lack of readiness" for treatment, resistance, or denial becomes the culprit. These practitioners usually give little thought to their practice approach or personal style and its impact on client "readiness" for treatment. They fail to examine the role their personal style, beliefs, attitudes, and practices have in creating the context that led to clients not succeeding in treatment.

Each practice theory and model has a relatively unique way of defining client problems, practitioner method and approach, interventions, and what constitutes successful outcome. For practitioners to believe that one theory or model is true, even if only for most people, they must believe in the universality of problems, methods and approaches, interventions, and successful outcome criteria. This contradicts the definition of theory. While being far from a concrete representation of the truth, a theory is a set of myths, expectations, guesses, and conjectures about what might be true (Best & Kellner, 1991). A theory is hypothetical; a set of ideas and explanations that need proving. No single theory can explain everything. According to Popper (1994), a theory ". . . always remains guesswork, and there is no theory that is not beset with problems" (p. 157). As such, treatment specialization can—although not always—encourage people to believe they have found the Truth where little truth exists.

Practitioners using an AMS perspective come to believe that some element of every established practice model, method, or theory may be helpful. Accordingly, every model, method, or theory can be adapted and used in a multi-systemic practice framework. As an AMS practitioner, one neither accepts any single model fully, nor disregards a model entirely if there is potential for helping a client succeed in a way that is compatible with professional social work values and ethics. These practitioners hone their critical thinking skills (Gambrill, 1997, 1990) and apply them in practice, particularly as it pertains to treatment theories, models, and methods. In the context of evidence-based practice (Cournoyer, 2004; Gibbs, 2003), sharpened critical thinking skills allow practitioners to closely read and evaluate practice theories, research, or case reports to recognize the strengths, weakness, and contradictions in theories, models, and/or policy related to social work practice.

Informed Eclecticism

The goal of AMS is for practitioners to develop an approach we call *informed eclecticism.* Informed eclecticism allows the use of multiple methods, interventions, and approaches in the context of practice that: (1) is held together by a perspective or approach that provides consistency, that makes practice choices in a way that makes sense in a particular client's life; and (2) is based, whenever possible, on the latest evidence about its efficacy with particular problems and particular clients. While it is often best to rely on empirical evidence, this data is in its infancy. AMS does not preclude the use of informed practice wisdom and personal creativity in developing intervention plans and approaches. It is up to practitioners to ensure that any treatment based in practice wisdom or that is creatively generated be discussed with colleagues, supervisors, or consultants to ensure theoretical consistency and that it fits within the code of professional ethics.

Informed eclecticism is different from the routine definition of eclecticism—the use of whatever theory, model, or method works best for their clients. While this is the goal of AMS practice specifically and social work practice in general (Timberlake, Farber, & Sabatino, 2002), it is an elusive goal indeed. Informed eclecticism often gets lost in a practitioner's quest to find something that "works." According to Gambrill (1997), eclecticism is "the view that we should adopt whatever theories or methodologies is useful in inquiry, no matter what their source and without worry about their consistency" (p. 93). The most important word in Gambrill's statement is "consistency." While there are practitioners who have managed to develop a consistent, organized, and holistic version of informed eclecticism, this is not the norm.

Too often, uninformed eclecticism resembles the following. A practitioner specializes by modality (individual therapy) and uses a variety of modality-specific ideas and practices in his work with clients; changing ideas and tactics when the approach he normally uses does not "work." This often leaves the practitioner searching (mostly in vain) for the magic intervention—what "works." Moreover, while uninformed eclectic practitioners use interventions from various "schools," they remain primarily wedded to one modality. Hence, they end up confusing themselves and their clients as they search for the "right" approach, rarely looking beyond their chosen modality and, therefore, never actually looking outside of their self-imposed, theoretical cage.

For example, an uninformed eclectic practitioner specializing in individual therapy may try a cognitive approach, a client-centered approach, a Freudian approach, or a behavioral approach. A family therapy specialist may use a structural, strategic, or solution-focused approach. However, in the end, little changes. These practitioners still believe that their clients need individual or family treatment. They rarely consider potentially useful ideas and tactics taken from different modalities that could be used instead of, or in combination with, an individual or family approach, mostly because they base treatment decisions on their chosen modality.

While informed eclecticism is the goal, most find it difficult to find consistency when trying to work from a variety of models at the same time. The informed eclectic practitioners, through experience and empirical evidence, have a unifying approach that serves as the basis for using different models or methods. What is important, according to clinical outcome research, is the consistency of approach in helping facilitate successful client outcome (Gaston, 1990; Miller & Rollnick, 2002; Harper & Lantz, 1996). Trying to be eclectic makes consistency (and treatment success), quite difficult.

What uninformed eclecticism lacks is the framework needed to gain a holistic and comprehensive understanding of the client in the context of his or her life, history, and multiple environments that leads naturally to culturally consistent treatment and intervention decisions. AMS, as it is described here, provides such a framework. It is holistic, integrative, ecological, and based in the latest empirical evidence. It is an inclusive framework that bases treatment decisions on a multi-systemic assessment of specific client history and culture. It is designed, whenever possible, to capitalize on client strengths, be consistent with culturally specific help-seeking behavior, and utilize existing or formulated community-based and/or natural support systems in the client's environment.

Defining Multi-Systemic Client Information

In this section we specifically discuss the different dimensions that comprise AMS practice. This is a general look at what constitutes multi-systemic client life information. There are six levels of information that, when integrated into a life history of clients, demonstrates how multiple theories, models, and approaches can be applied to better understand, assess, and treat clients or client-systems. Generally, the six dimensions (biological, psychological, family, religious/spiritual/existential, social/environmental, and macro) encompass range of information needed to complete a comprehensive, multi-systemic assessment, treatment, and intervention plan with client-systems of all sizes and configurations.

1. Biological Dimension

AMS practitioners need to understand what some have called the "mind-body connection," or the links between social/emotional, behavioral, and potential biological or genetic issues that may be, at least in part, driving the problems presented by clients in practice. As scientific evidence mounts regarding the biological and genetic sources of personal troubles (i.e., some mental illness, etc.), it grows imperative for well-trained AMS practitioners to apply this knowledge in everyday work with clients (Ginsberg, Nackerud, & Larrison, 2004). The responsibility for understanding biology and physical health goes well beyond those working in direct healthcare practice settings (i.e., hospital, HIV, or hospice practice settings). Issues pertaining to physical health confront practitioners in all practice settings.

For example, practitioners working in mental health settings are confronted daily with issues pertaining to human biology; the sources and determinants of mental illness, differential uses of psychotropic medication, and often, the role played in client behavior by proper nutrition, appropriate health care, and even physical rest. In foster care and/or family preservation, practitioners also confront the effects of parental abuses (i.e., fetal alcohol syndrome [FAS]), medication management, and child/adolescent physical and biological development issues.

Beyond learning about the potential biological or physical determinants of various client troubles, having a keen understanding of the potential physical and health risks associated with various behaviors and/or lifestyles places practitioners in the position of intervening to save lives. For example, practitioners working with substance abusing or chemically dependent clients must understand drug pharmacology—especially drug-mixing—to predict potentially life threatening physical withdrawal effects and/or to prevent intentional or unintentional harm caused by drug overdose (Johnson, 2004).

AMS requires that practitioners keep current with the latest information about human biology, development, genetics, and potential associated health risks facing clients and client-systems in practice. With that knowledge, practitioners can include this information during client assessment, treatment planning, and intervention strategies. It also requires practitioners to know the limits of professional responsibility. That is, social workers are not physicians and should never offer medical advice or guidance that is not supported by properly trained physicians. Therefore, AMS practitioners utilize the appropriate medical professionals as part of assessment, planning, and intervention processes with all clients.

2. Psychological/Emotional Dimension

AMS practitioners need a working knowledge of the ways that psychological and emotional functioning are intertwined with clients' problems and strengths, how issues from this dimension contribute to the way their client or client-system interacts with self and others in their environment, and how their environments influence their psychological and emotional functioning. There are several important skill sets that practitioners must develop to consider issues in this dimension. First, being able to recognize potential problems through a mental screening examination is a skill necessary to all practitioners. Also, having a keen understanding of the *Diagnostic and Statistical Manual of Mental Disorders* (DSM) (American Psychological Association, 2000), including the multi-axial diagnostic process, and recognition of the limits of this tool in the overall multi-systemic assessment process is instrumental. Especially critical is the ability to recognize co-occurring disorders (Johnson, 2004). It is also valuable to learn the Person-in-Environment (PIE) assessment system (Karls & Wandrei, 1994a, 1994b), a diagnostic model developed specifically for social workers to incorporate environmental influences.

In addition to understanding how psychology and emotion affects client mood and behavior, AMS practitioners also know how to employ different theories and models used for treating psychological and emotional functioning problems in the context of a client's multi-systemic assessment and treatment plan. This includes methods of treating individuals, families, and groups. Depending on the client's multi-systemic assessment, each of these modalities or some combination of modalities is appropriate for people with problems in this dimension.

3. Family Dimension

The family is the primary source of socialization, modeling, and nurturing of children. Hence, the family system has a significant impact on people's behavior, and people's behavior has significant impact on the health and well-being of their family system (Johnson, 2004). By integrating a family systems perspective into AMS, practitioners will often be able to make sense of behavior attitudes, beliefs, and values that would otherwise be difficult to understand or explain.

For our purposes, a family is defined as a group of people—regardless of their actual blood or legal relationship—whom clients consider to be members of their family (Johnson, 2004). This definition is designed to privilege clients' perceptions and subjective construction of reality and avoid disagreements over who is or is not in someone's family. So, if a client refers to a neighbor as "Uncle Joe," then that perception represents their reality. What good would it do to argue otherwise? Just as in client engagement discussed earlier, AMS practitioners seek to understand and embrace their client's unique definition of family, rather than imposing a rigid standard that may not fit their perceived reality. This is especially important when dealing with gay and lesbian clients. The law may not recognize gay or lesbian marriage, but AMS practitioners must, if that is the nature of the client's relationship and consistent with their belief system.

It is important to have a working knowledge of different theories and approaches to assessing and treating families and couples, as well as the ability to construct three-generation genograms to help conceptualize family systems and characterize the relationships that exist within the family system and between the family and its environment. Family treatment requires unique skills, specialized post-graduate training, and regular supervision before a practitioner can master the methods and call herself a "family therapist." However, the journey toward mastery is well worth it. Family treatment can be among the most effective and meaningful treatment modalities, often used in conjunction with other modalities (individual and/or group treatment), or as the primary treatment method.

4. Religious/Spiritual/Existential Dimension

Practitioners, students, and social work educators are often wary of exploring issues related to religion and spirituality in practice or the classroom. While there are exceptions, this important dimension often goes unexamined. Exploring people's religious beliefs and/or the tenets of their faith, even if they do not appear to have faith of spiritual beliefs, as they pertain to people's subjective definition of self in relation to the world is an important part of AMS practice.

How clients view themselves in relation to others and their world provides an interesting window into the inner workings of their individual interpretation of culture. The extent that clients have internalized messages (positive, negative, and/or neutral) about their behavior from their faith community or personal spiritual belief systems can lead to an understanding of why people approach their lives and others in the ways they do. Moreover, much can be learned, based on these beliefs, about people's belief in the potential for change, how change occurs, and whom is best suited to help in that change process (if anyone at all), especially as it relates to the many moral and religious messages conveyed about people with problems.

Examination of this dimension goes beyond discovering which church or synagogue clients attend. It is designed to learn how and by what means clients define themselves and their lives in their worlds. What tenets they use to justify their lives, and how these tenets either support their current lives or not can be used to help lead them toward change. There is much to be learned about client culture, how people interpret their culture in daily life, and how they view their life in their personal context from an examination of their religious or spiritual beliefs.

Moreover, religious and spiritual belief systems can also be a source of strength and support when considered in treatment plans. For example, while many clients may benefit from attendance at a community support group (i.e., Alcoholics Anonymous, Overeaters Anonymous, etc.) or professional treatment, some will benefit even more from participation in groups and events through local houses of worship. In our experience, many clients unable to succeed in professional treatment or support groups found success through a connection or reconnection with organizations that share their faith, whatever that faith may be.

5. Social/Environmental Dimension

Beyond the individual and family, AMS practitioners look to the client's community, including the physical environment, for important clues to help with engagement, assessment, and intervention planning. People live in communities comprised of three different types: (1) location (neighborhoods, cities, and rural or urban villages), (2) identification (religion, culture, race, etc.), and (3) affiliation (group memberships, subcultures, professional, political/ ideological groups, etc.). There are five subdimensions that comprise the social/environmental dimension and incorporate the three types of communities listed above (Johnson, 2004):

1. Local community. This includes learning about physical environment, living conditions, a person's fit within her community, neighborhoods, where and how people live on a daily basis, and how they believe they are treated and/or accepted by community members and the community's power structure (i.e., the police, etc.).

2. Cultural context. This includes learning about clients' larger culture, their individual interpretation of culture, and how it drives or influences their daily life. Also included here is an exploration of histories of oppression and discrimination (individual, family, and community) and a client's subcultural group membership (i.e., drug culture, gang culture, etc.).

3. Social class. Often overlooked by practitioners, "information about people's social class is directly related to information about their families, the goodness-of-fit between the person and environment, and the strengths, resources, and/or barriers in their communities" (Johnson, 2004, p. 226). Some believe that no other demographic factor explains so extensively the differences between people and/or groups (Lipsitz, 1997; Davis & Proctor, 1989). Social class represents a combination of income, education, occupation, prestige, and community. It encompasses how these factors affect people's relative wealth and access to power and opportunity (Johnson, 2004).

4. Social/relational. Human beings are social creatures who define themselves in relation to others (Johnson, 2004). Therefore, it is necessary to know something about people's ability to relate to others in their social environment. This investigation includes loved ones, friends, peers, supervisors, teachers, and others that they relate to in their daily life.

5. Legal history and involvement. Obviously, this subdimension includes information about involvement with the legal system, by the client, family members, and friends and peers. More than recording a simple demographic history, seek to discover their feelings, attitudes, and beliefs about themselves, their place in the world, and how their brushes with the law fit into or influence their worldview.

6. Community resources. Investigate the nature and availability of organizational support, including the role of social service organizations, politics, and your presence as a social worker in a client's life. For example, can clients find a program to serve their needs, or what does seeing a social worker mean within their community or culture? What are the conditions of the schools and the influence of churches, neighborhood associations, and block clubs? More importantly, what is the prevailing culture of the local environment? Are neighbors supportive or afraid of each other, and can a client expect to reside in the present situation and receive the support needed to change?

Be sure to include the professional helping system in this subdimension. Practitioners, their agencies, and the policies that assist or impede the professional helping process join with client-systems as part of the overall system in treatment. In other words, we must consider ourselves as part of the system—we do not stand outside in objective observation. This includes practitioner qualities and styles, agency policies, broader policies related to specific populations, and reimbursement policies, including managed care. All of these factors routinely influence the extent to which clients receive help, how clients are perceived in the helping system and, in the case of reimbursement policies, the method of treatment clients are eligible to receive regardless of how their multi-systemic assessment turns out.

Familiarity with various theories and models of community provide the keys to understanding the role of the social, physical, political, and economic environment in an individual's life. Community models look at the broader environment and its impact on people. Clients or client-systems with issues located in this dimension often respond well to group and family treatment methods. Occasionally, practitioners will be required to intervene at the local neighborhood or community level through organizing efforts and/or personal or political advocacy. For example:

> I (Johnson) was treating a client in individual and occasional family treatment when it was discovered that the daughter had been molested by a neighbor. The parents had not reported the molestation. I soon learned that this neighbor was rumored to have molested several young girls in the neighborhood and that nobody was willing to report the molestations. I urged my client to organize a neighborhood meeting of all involved parents at her home. I served as the group facilitator for an intense meeting

that ultimately built the community support needed to involve law enforcement. Within days, all of the parents in this group met with law enforcement. The perpetrator was arrested, convicted, and sentenced to life imprisonment.

6. Macro Dimension

AMS practitioners do not stop looking for relevant client information at the local level. They also look for clues in the way that macro issues influence clients, their problems, and potential for change. Knowledge of various laws (local, state, and national) are critical, as well as an understanding of how various social policies are interpreted and enforced in a particular client's life. For example, AMS requires an understanding of how child welfare policies affect the life of a chemically depend-ent mother, how healthcare policy affects a family's decisions about seeking med-ical treatment for their children, or how local standards of hygiene or cleanliness affect a family's status and acceptance in their community.

Issues to consider at this level also include public sentiment, stereotypes, and mechanisms of oppression that play a significant role in the lives of people who are not Caucasian, male, middle-class (or more affluent) citizens. Racism, classism, homophobia, and sexism, to name a few, are real threats to people who are attempt-ing to live a "normal" life. An AMS practitioner must understand this reality and learn from clients what their individual perceptions are of these mechanisms and how they affect their problems and potential for change. The macro dimension involves issues such as housing, employment, and public support, along with the dynamics of the criminal justice system. For example, if clients have been arrested for domestic violence, what is the chance they will get fair and just legal represen-tation? If they have been convicted and served jail or prison sentences, what are the chances they will have a reasonable chance of finding sufficient employment upon release?

These issues can be addressed in individual, family, or group treatments. Often, group treatment is an effective way to address issues clients struggle with at the macro level. Group treatment provides clients a way to address these issues in the context of mutual social support and a sense of belonging, helping them realize that they are not alone in their struggles (Yalom, 1995). AMS practitioners also rec-ognize the need for political advocacy and community organizing methods for clients who present with consistent struggles with issues at the macro level.

Summary

The hallmark of AMS is its reliance on and integration of multi-systemic client information into one comprehensive assessment, treatment, and intervention plan. It incorporates knowledge, skills, and values from multiple sources, and relies on var-ious sources of knowledge to paint a holistic picture of people's lives, struggles, strengths and resources, and potentials for change. Practitioners need a current working knowledge of human behavior, social systems theories, the latest social research and practice evaluation results, the impact of public laws and policies, as well as the skills and abilities to plan and implement treatment approaches as needed, in a manner consistent with our definition of informed eclecticism.

Many students new to AMS start out confused because the requirements seem so diverse and complicated. However, as you will see in the case presentations to follow, an organized and efficient practitioner who has learned to think and act multi-systemically can gather large amounts of critically important information about a client in a relatively short period. For this to happen, you must have a deep understanding of various theories, models, and practice approaches that address the various systemic levels considered and be willing to accept that no single model is completely right or wrong. It is always easier to latch on to one model and "go with it." However, the goal of practice is not to be correct or to promote your own ease and comfort, but to develop an assessment and treatment plan that is right for each client, whether or not you would ever use it in your own life. Social work practice is not about the social worker, but the client. It is important never to lose sight of this fact.

Bibliography

American Psychiatric Association (2000). *Diagnostic and statistical manual of mental disorders* (4th ed., TR). Washington, DC: Author.

Appleby, G. A. (2001). Dynamics of oppression and discrimination. In G. A. Appleby, E. Colon, & J. Hamilton (eds.), *Diversity, oppression, and social functioning: Person-in-environment assessment and intervention.* Boston: Allyn and Bacon.

Best, S., & Kellner, D. (1991). *Postmodern theory: Critical interrogations.* New York: Guilford Press.

Cournoyer, B. R. (2004). *The evidence-based social work skills book.* Boston: Allyn and Bacon.

Cox, E. O., & Parsons, R. J. (1994). *Empowerment-oriented social work practice with the elderly.* Pacific Grove, CA: Brooks/Cole.

Davis, L. E., & Proctor, E. K. (1989). *Race, gender, and class: Guidelines for practice with individuals, families, and groups.* Englewood Cliffs, NJ: Prentice-Hall.

Derezotes, D. S. (2000). *Advanced generalist social work practice.* Thousand Oaks, CA: Sage.

Fong, R. (2001). Culturally competent social work practice: Past and present. In R. Fong & S. Furuto (eds.), *Culturally competent practice: Skills, interventions, and evaluations.* Boston: Allyn and Bacon.

Freire, P. (1993). *Pedagogy of the oppressed.* New York: Continuum.

Gambrill, E. (1997). *Social work practice: A critical thinker's guide.* New York: Oxford University Press.

Gambrill, E. (1990). *Critical thinking in clinical practice.* San Francisco: Jossey-Bass.

Gaston, L. (1990). The concept of the alliance and its role in psychotherapy: Theoretical and empirical considerations. *Psychotherapy, 27,* 143–153.

Geertz, C. (1973). *The interpretation of cultures.* New York: Basic Books.

Germain, C. B., & Gitterman, A. (1996). *The life model of social work practice* (2nd ed.). New York: Columbia University Press.

Germain, C. B., & Gitterman, A. (1980). *The ecological model of social work practice.* New York: Columbia University Press.

Gibbs, L. E. (2003). *Evidence-based practice for the helping professions: A practical guide with integrated multimedia.* Pacific Grove, CA: Brooks/Cole.

Ginsberg, L., Nackerud, L., & Larrison, C. R. (2004). *Human biology for social workers: Development, ecology, genetics, and health.* Boston: Allyn and Bacon.

GlenMaye, L. (1998). Empowerment of women. In L. M. Gutierrez, R. J. Parsons, & E. O. Cox (eds.), *Empowerment in social work practice: A sourcebook.* Pacific Grove, CA: Brooks/Cole.

Gordon, J. U. (1993). A culturally specific approach to ethnic minority young adults. In E. M. Freeman (ed.), *Substance abuse treatment: A family systems perspective.* Newbury Park, CA: Sage.

Greif, G. L. (1986). The ecosystems perspective "meets the press." *Social Work, 31,* 225–226.

Harper, K. V., & Lantz, J. (1996). *Cross-cultural practice: Social work practice with diverse populations.* Chicago: Lyceum Books.

Johnson, J. L. (2004). *Fundamentals of substance abuse practice.* Pacific Grove, CA: Brooks/Cole.

Johnson, J. L. (2000). *Crossing borders—Confronting history: Intercultural adjustment in a post–Cold War world.* Lanham, MD: University Press of America.

Karls, J., & Wandrei, K. (1994a). *Person-in-environment system: The PIE classification system for functioning problems.* Washington, DC: NASW.

Karls, J., & Wandrei, K. (1994b). *PIE manual: Person-in-environment system: The PIE classification system for social functioning.* Washington, DC: NASW.

Kozol, J. (1991). *Savage inequalities: Children in America's schools.* New York: Crown Publishers.

Leigh, J. W. (1998). *Communicating for cultural competence.* Boston: Allyn and Bacon.

Lipsitz, G. (1997). Class and class consciousness: Teaching about social class in public universities. In A. Kumar (ed.), *Class issues.* New York: New York University Press.

Longres, J. F. (2000). *Human behavior in the social environment* (3rd ed.). Itasca, IL: F. E. Peacock.

Lum, D. (1999). *Culturally competent practice.* Pacific Grove, CA: Brooks/Cole.

McLaren, P. (1995). *Critical pedagogy and predatory culture: Oppositional politics in a postmodern era.* London: Routledge.

Miley, K. K., O'Melia, M., & DuBois, B. (2004). *Generalist social work practice: An empowerment approach.* Boston: Allyn and Bacon.

Miller, W. R., & Rollnick, S. (2002). *Motivational interviewing: Preparing people to change addictive behavior* (2nd ed.). New York: Guilford Press.

Mills, C. W. (1959). *The sociological imagination.* New York: Oxford University Press.

Parsons, R. J., Gutierrez, L. M., & Cox, E. O. (1998). A model for empowerment practice. In L. M. Gutierrez, R. J. Parsons, & E. O. Cox (eds.), *Empowerment in social work practice: A sourcebook.* Pacific Grove, CA: Brooks/Cole.

Pinderhughes, E. (1989). *Understanding race, ethnicity, and power.* New York: Free Press.

Popper, K. R. (1994). *The myth of the framework: In defense of science and rationality.* Edited by M. A. Notturno. New York: Routledge.

Saleebey, D. (2002). *The strengths perspective in social work practice* (3rd ed.). Boston: Allyn and Bacon.

Smelser, N. J. (1992). Culture: Coherent or incoherent. In R. Munch & N. J. Smelser (eds.), *Theory of culture.* Berkeley, CA: University of California Press.

Timberlake, E. M., Farber, M. Z., & Sabatino, C. A. (2002). *The general method of social work practice: McMahon's generalist perspective* (4th ed.). Boston: Allyn and Bacon.

van Wormer, K., & Davis, D. R. (2003). *Addiction treatment: A strengths perspective.* Pacific Grove, CA: Brooks/Cole.

Yalom, I. (1995). *The theory and practice of group psychotherapy* (4th ed.). New York: Basic Books.

2

Golem, Albania

Kristi J. Gleeson

Introduction

Golem is a small, bustling, muddy, determined village about forty kilometers outside of Tirana, the capital city of Albania. One of the last Eastern European countries to emerge from Communism, in the early 1990s Albania was full of hope and optimism in the years immediately following the fall of the former government. However, with the baggage of over fifty years of brutal repression and no experience with free market economies and/or democracy, the country's three million citizens were destitute, existing on the slippery slope of chaos and anarchy. In 1997, the first democratically elected government resigned in the aftermath of a countrywide "pyramid scheme" that robbed most Albanians of most of their personal finances. The collapse of the pyramid schemes burst what many were calling the "Albania economic miracle" of the mid to late 1990s. Albania and its citizens crashed back to Earth, as it were.

Recovery was slow. By 2003, per capita income was less than US $100 per month and Albania's economy and social infrastructure was fragile. While Tirana developed quickly from 1990 through 2003, the smaller cities, villages, and rural areas struggled with high unemployment, crumbling infrastructure, and electrical shortages that left most of the population without power for up to twenty hours a day.

Golem is one of these villages. In any other country, being located on the national highway in a "tourist" zone would be beneficial, leading to rapid development. Yet, in Golem, half-built hotels, trash filled beaches on a raw, sewage-infested sea, abandoned cars littering the landscape, and the partially constructed houses of internal migrants forced into internal exile by the former Communist regime made Golem a village with significant problems.

Questions

As an American social worker preparing to work in Albania, it is important to understand the history and culture of the country (Johnson, 1999). Albania is an interesting country with interesting peoples. Before moving on, please respond to the following questions and exercises. You may want to respond in small groups to increase the learning potential.

1. Find diverse literatures about Albania, its people, and culture. Focus your inquiry on Albania's history, beginning with World War I to the present. In two or three pages, prepare a "sketch" of the history and culture of this country. Be sure to include as part of your discussion any religious influences in the country.

2. Find literature about their former dictator, Enver Hoxha. Describe Albanian Communism under Hoxha, and differentiate their brand of Communism from the Soviet Union and People's Republic of China.

3. Search for information pertaining to the Albanian pyramid scandals of the late 1990s. The World Bank has a plethora of information about this period. What happened and how has it been resolved?

4. Describe Albania today, culturally and economically. Use U.S. State Department literature and information from other sources to paint a picture of this country and its people.

Albanian Statehood

To understand Albania at the community level, it is necessary to understand Albania as a state. The Communist dictator Enver Hoxha ruled Albania ruthlessly from 1945 until his death in 1986. Yet, his harsh legacy lives on. Hoxha's conservative brand of a strict Stalinist form of Communism and the resultant paranoia led Albania into isolation from the rest of the world, beginning in 1977. In the early 1960s, Albania abandoned its ties with the Soviet Union during Khrushchev's post-Stalinist reform era and then in 1977 it abandoned ties with the People's Republic of China during Deng Xiao Ping's post-Maoist reform era.

The Hoxha regime allowed few outsiders into the country and even fewer Albanians out of the country. The Albanian people were deliberately and effectively isolated from the rest of Europe and the world for almost half a century. As the outside world developed and changed, life stood still in Albania. In the countryside, life remained similar to how it was in the nineteenth century. In much of the country, it remains that way today.

When "democracy" and democratic movements took root in Albania in 1992, Albania was little more than a collection of decrepit, nonfunctioning factories, roads full of holes, fewer than 800 automobiles, homes with no electricity, and more often than not, no running water. It was comprised of people and newly emerging government reformers with no concept of democracy and/or free market capitalism. Despite the significant problems, Albania was also comprised of warm and generous people, full of humor and determination to join the modern world. Albania's problem was that nobody in the country had the experience to lead the transformation, resulting in significant problems that peaked during the pyramid scandals of 1997. This period was marked by total economic collapse, the sacking of its existing government, and, for a time, chaos, and anarchy.

Questions

Now that you have learned more about Albania, its culture, history, and people, it's time to prepare for your work. Please answer the following questions, either alone or in small groups.

1. What language do Albanian's speak? Will your native language (English) be helpful there, or will you have language barriers to overcome. What considerations or arrangements must you make to help with your work?

2. On an Albanian map, find Golem. Describe its location. Can you find any specific information about this city or region?

3. Earlier, the author mentioned that many of Golem's citizens were "internal migrants." Based on what you learned about Albania's Communist past, what does the term "internal migrant" mean in Albania?

Assessment Information

Most of Golem's 3,000 inhabitants had graduated from middle or high school. Golem was similar to the rest of Albania. Its people had a high literacy rate and a well-educated population. In this region, most people were farmers, working the fields around Golem to produce fruit and vegetables for sale in Durres, the country's second largest city and major seaport.

Golem's community resources included the commune (village) office, an elementary school, a post office, a small health center, and a mosque. Golem had no local media. The streets contained a few small coffee bars and corner stores. However, Golem was a determined and self-labeled "curious" population with a "practical sense of problem solving."

In Golem, as in the rest of Albania, the sense of family was strong. Albania has a long "clan" history that remained stronger in the north than in the remainder of the country. Yet, even in the country's middle and south, family connections and relationships are paramount. That is, Albanians place family and family order above all. Family interests come before individual and/or community interests.

Albania is also a patriarchal culture. The father is the absolute head of the household and married daughters often must live with the husband's family. In the Albanian tradition, family and blood connections give citizens their sense of belonging, cultural definitions, and their sense of importance and place in the world.

However, the intense loyalty that personifies families does not usually extend beyond the family system. This is especially true since the end of the Communist period. Any feeling of community and/or "civic duty" that existed had begun to rebound only recently, and it was weak at best. During the Communist era, neighbors spied on neighbors; friends betrayed friends. Even in-laws were suspect within the family. Albanians still mention that one out of every four is a suspected informer. Only blood could be trusted.

Moreover, during the Communist period, citizens had to "volunteer" for community or neighborhood projects each week, such as street cleaning. Hence, any efforts toward enlisting volunteer civic involvement were met with suspicion or labeled as "Communist propaganda." The Albanian Communist system destroyed feelings of community, forcing communities into their fundamental parts (family groups) as perhaps the only way to survive and avoid being labeled a spy or enemy of the state.

Today the situation is slightly different. While people do not fear their neighbors anymore, attitudes have swung to indifference. "If it doesn't concern me or my family, then I don't really care about it" is a typical attitude. Whereas in the United States you could (without too much difficulty) rally your friends and neighbors to protest against a mayor's embezzling of community funds, in Albania the same situation would be met with apathy. "He's already left with our money to Italy, what can we do about it now? That's the way it is and probably always will be."

On a national or macro-level, indifference often becomes ignorance. Although democratically elected, Albania's leaders have little experience with democracy and often choose their ministers and cabinet members based on friendship and family ties rather than on experience or ability. In the countryside, people rarely know their rights, hardly know by name their elected representatives, and do not believe they could have any affect on national policy, even if they knew what national policy was. Elected officials, both on the local (Commune) level and at the national level, have little feel for being "public servants" and rarely even ask their constituents what they want or need.

Questions

The negative attitude of the Albanian people toward community involvement portrayed by the author is common in formerly Communist states. Any evidence or suggestion of volunteer work or community assistance is often met with suspicion or dismissed as Communist propaganda. Yet, international organizations send community organizers into these countries in an effort to overcome these problems. Assume for a moment that you are the organizer sent to Golem and respond to the following questions.

1. Based on the community practice literature, what issues would you expect to encounter when you arrive?

2. **What strategies would you employ to recruit and motivate citizens to participate?**

3. **Based on the literature, how would you proceed to effectively confront and overcome the issues leftover from the Communist period?**

4. **What strategies would you use to engage these people in community action, and how would you deal with the inevitable issues and barriers they would face in their efforts?**

Locating the Willing

Out of this indifference and brutal history came nine citizens of Golem who decided they wanted to make a difference and work together to improve their community. With help from an international nongovernmental organization (NGO) I worked with, these nine citizens formed a group committed to improving their community. They met every two weeks to learn about democracy, human rights, women's issues, the Albanian constitution, and community organizing. Two field coordinators from our NGO who were well trained in community organizing facilitated these meetings. This was my role in Golem.

We located and recruited the nine people through local contacts, political connections, and family relationships. My Albanian colleague was able to locate extended family and friends in the area that were willing to help us locate willing participants. We talked to people in their homes, cafés, restaurants, and on street corners. Our task was to demonstrate to them that this effort was different from before. Unlike the past, we needed to convince the citizens that their efforts were a central part of self-rule and an emerging sense of self-determination. During Communist times, their "volunteer" work was in total service of the Communist regime, whether they liked or agreed with it or not. Now, for the first time in memory, citizens could shape their community consistent with their vision, not the government's.

From our grassroots efforts, nine committed citizens came forward ready to assume community leadership. Their willingness to volunteer precipitated a series of meetings that involved education, tactics, and strategies. After a full year of learning and discussion, they were ready to act.

Our citizen group decided to focus on resolving a major issue in their community: Golem's lack of drinking water. The people of Golem had been without potable water in their homes for over three years; in fact, no water flowed from the tap. Every few days, Golem's women and children would walk a far distance to gather water for cooking, cleaning, and drinking. The community group decided to advocate for the return of drinking water in Golem.

Usually, I recommend new community groups choose a series of easier tasks in the beginning to build group cohesiveness and confidence. When they decided to approach this issue, I was privately worried that it was too big for a group of citizens used to waiting for their government to act. Remember, for at least fifty years Albanian citizens did not take initiative in their communities. During Communist times, that would have been dangerous. Hence, I worried that their group might unravel at the first sign of resistance. Yet, this was their decision, and I supported their efforts from the beginning.

Client Engagement

The group of nine was sometimes apprehensive and reluctant to engage in an effort that "conventional" Albanian wisdom suggested was hopeless. These brave citizens were surrounded by people who did not have a sense of community, people who had never felt the power of working together in collaboration toward a community goal. The word "volunteer" did not have a benevolent meaning. Instead, it reminded people of Communist times when political and criminal prisoners were forced to perform lethal "volunteer" work in Albania's perilous chromium mines. It was difficult to engage Golem's citizens to give up their free time and work for something that would be, in reality, difficult to achieve. They had many reasons not to commit to a goal, not to engage or become involved in a community project. In Golem, these issues usually fell into three categories: time, hope, and money.

Golem's poor farmers spent most of their time in the fields planting and harvesting crops or in their houses trying to stretch their meager budget to feed and clothe their family. Women worked full time in the fields, only to come home and cook, clean, and raise children. It was difficult to convince people struggling to survive from day to day to join a community group for no pay. On the other hand, if unemployment was high, people usually had more free time on their hands. With the majority of Golem's population being farmers and spending long hours in their fields, most did not want to spend their few free hours "working" with an NGO and not getting paid for it.

Generally, soon after undertaking community efforts, people begin realizing that their efforts needed money—more money than the people ever thought possible to raise. This realization often makes people give up hope before beginning such an effort. Even if the Commune office decided to help, it did not have nearly enough money to fix the problem. For many, this was enough reason not to join the fight.

Alinsky (1972) believes that successful community organizing involves developing community power, either real or threatened. I believe that there are generally two sources of power in community organization: money and/or numbers (Johnson, 1999). While it is generally best to have both, either a well-funded effort without large numbers of an underfunded effort with larger numbers of people has a chance to succeed. Hence, given the economic issues in Albania and the difficulty finding outside donors, our strategy—at least in the beginning—was to build our numbers. However, this is more difficult than you might think.

Fifty years of Communism, twelve years of post-Communist poverty, broken promises, corrupt leaders, incompetent local authorities, fatalism, and despair led most people to quit before they even started. Golem is no different in this respect then the rest of Albania. Many Albanians have lost hope. Even the citizens that participated in the project felt hopeless periodically. Our field coordinators labeled their hopelessness as the group feeling "suspicious" about our motives. The group's suspiciousness plagued the project; even our field coordinators felt the community group's goals could not meet with success.

So how does a whole community become engaged in a project that will take time they do not want to give, money they do not have, and a faith in themselves they do not seem to possess? Patience is the operating word in community circumstances such as Golem. Our experience taught us that the hardest part of community organizing occurs in the beginning, when the task is to convince people to participate and that they can make a difference. Convincing them takes time. In fact, early in the project this task comprised the majority of our time. Our field coordinators spent most of their time talking to the butchers, shopkeepers, and teachers in Golem, trying to convince them to become part of the project by committing their time and energy toward the greater good.

Once people agreed to attend biweekly meetings, our first strategy was to start small. It would have been too difficult to organize a large community event immediately. We started with what we called "information gathering and sharing." In the beginning, we only had nine people willing to participate. We suggested that community development is not about receiving huge donations from international sources and rebuilding an orphanage or a school. We talked about community development in terms of involving community members in everyday activities that work to strengthen their social bonds and improve their daily lives. The community should do the transformational work for itself and not expect outsiders to make it happen.

Our field coordinators and the nine citizens first worked to educate themselves about Golem's problems and community resources; and then worked to educate the rest of Golem's citizens. Group members were encouraged to talk to their neighbors about what they learned and to become the project's recruiters. We realized that the community organizing process proceeded when participants shared our discussions of the issues and suggested solutions with other community members. Neighbors and friends recruiting neighbors and friends was our most effective recruitment tool.

Our second strategy was to get this small group of people doing something on their own behalf; it did not matter what they did, as long as the group took action. People will not participate past the first meeting if they must sit through meetings without much interaction or doing anything. Their time was important and we needed to ensure that the original participants learned that their time would be spent acting on their community's behalf.

Hence, we had members making flyers and passing them out, going to the Commune office to request information about a law or a recent official decision that concerned the village, or talking to five different people about an issue. These are examples of the small actions we asked the participants to perform in order to get them involved and feeling as if they are contributing. We called these activities "small steps."

Sometimes, the field coordinators grew frustrated by doing seemingly small tasks. What they did not realize was that if small steps were successful (and they usually are, if they are small enough), the success builds encouragement, hope, and confidence. This generally leads to a group's ability to take bigger steps and realize larger successes. Our group of citizens in Golem started talking to their mayor, spreading information all over the community, attending village council meetings, and organizing meetings with members of the community and local leaders.

Another strategy we used to engage people was to ask the already involved citizens to bring their spouses, cousins, parents, siblings, and friends to the next meeting or activity. In Albania, where information can be hard to come by, and therefore has a tendency to be hoarded, it was amazing how many people never thought to tell their spouse about what they had learned or what they were doing, no matter how trivial or exciting. However, if everyone brought one additional person to the next meeting, our group would instantly double.

This was our main strategy: to build power through numbers.

To find a strong core group of people in Golem to form the foundation of the community group took about one month. Our field coordinators first went to the village elder[1] to present their ideas about Golem. They asked the elders for two things: permission to start a community group in the village and the names of "people with good reputations" to contact and talk with about the project. After the elder granted permission and provided the names, the field coordinators went around the village literally "selling" the project. They talked with everyone and anyone they could. Shopkeepers, teachers, the woman walking her cow down the road—anyone willing to listen was invited to the first meeting.

At this point, the community workers served as "salespeople" and recruiters. They used "cold calling" methods including knocking on doors and visiting businesses soliciting support and participation. They also used a "snowball" method for recruitment. Once they found an interested person, the workers asked for the names of other people in the village who might also be interested. The workers also used their own personal connections in the villages. One of the core group members, a teacher, was a close friend of our field coordinator and offered the use of his classroom as a meeting place for the group.

The field coordinators spent two days talking to people in Golem. Everyone was invited to the first meeting, set for three days later (people tended to lose interest or forget if the meeting was too many days later). They spoke with approximately two hundred people; about thirty-five came to the first meeting. At this meeting, the workers explained the project and exchanged ideas about issues the community faced and possible solutions to these issues. Three weeks later, the group shrunk to twelve members committed to the project and nine considered "core" members. Golem's community group was ready to take on their first project.

---

[1]The village elder is not an elected position, but usually is a designated male between 40–60 years old who holds a high position of respect in the community. The village elder is responsible for the overall well-being of the village and may or may not collaborate with the local elected representatives. To begin to work in a community without first consulting the elder is a serious breech of etiquette and could lead to the failure of the project.

During the process of engagement, we connected with the inhabitants of Golem. We were careful to make professional (not personal) connections with the people we worked with in Golem. As we learned more about Golem, about their hardships and victories, about the difficulties of their daily lives, the more we wanted to help them learn to help themselves. I encouraged our staff to open up to the citizens about themselves, about their own triumphs and losses as a way of helping the people of Golem come to trust us and believe in the project and the possibility of success. We tried being as open and honest as possible with the citizens.

We had to answer difficult questions such as, "where else in Albania do you work and have there been other projects that have failed?" This also meant working during the times when the citizens had free time for village meetings, such as in the evening after they finished working in the fields. In this way, our field coordinators in a sense became part of the community and the people of Golem came to trust them and work more closely with them. However, there was always the danger of opening up too much and/or becoming too attached. In Golem, we detached ourselves enough not to get too involved but still develop trust and have the ability to lead the process of community development.

Cultural Competence

The longer we worked in Golem, the more we learned the issues of the community that were barriers to success. We helped uncover three main issues: an inability to problem-solve or strategize, a lack of follow-through, and an attitude of "do it for me." We felt these were the main issues that had paralyzed the community and created an inability to help themselves.

When the water stopped running in people's homes over three years before, a few citizens went to the mayor to complain. The mayor replied, "What can I do? I don't have water either." The citizens promptly gave up and went home. They had not taken any action since to get water flowing in their homes again. Another example was the large amount of trash on the ground in the village. During Communist times, it was someone's job to clean up the garbage. After Communism collapsed, no longer was someone responsible for trash collection and it piled up on the ground all over the village. Although everyone complained about the trash, nobody made an effort to pick it up, not even on their own front sidewalks. During the planning stage, the citizens were unable to suggest any other ideas than to request an international donor to pay for a major water engineering project.

Although we never discovered why there was a lack of follow-through, we thought perhaps it stemmed from a lack of hope or from disbelief that the project would work. We theorized that the lack of problem-solving skills and inability to strategize stemmed from Albania's Communist past, and the overall education system. The educational system in Albania is based on rote learning. That is, the teacher lectures and the students write it down in order to repeat it back on examinations. Critical thinking and analytical skills are not addressed or taught. Communism taught people (by force) to follow orders without thinking. This past slowly sapped people's ability and desire to think for themselves. Questioning orders or challenging authority led to punishment, jail time, or worse.

The "do it for me" attitude was a direct outcome of the Kosovo Crisis. We learned through talking with the community that during and after the crisis in Kosovo (1999), which sent thousands of refugees flooding into Albania, hundreds of international NGOs sent people and money to help the refugees and allow the Albanians themselves to help the refugees. This created a culture of organizations rebuilding schools, libraries, and health centers quickly and efficiently, but without community input. An organization would come to a village; three weeks and thousands of dollars later, a new health center would appear. It did not seem to matter that there were no doctors in the village and no supplies to stock the new health center.

The result of this huge influx of money was that communities learned to ask for and expect thousands of dollars in grant money without any input. Unfortunately, earthquakes, hurricanes, and wars in other parts of the world diverted much of this money away from Albania, leaving many of the projects half-finished or finished quickly with lower quality. We learned from experience that community development projects without community involvement are not successful because citizens do not feel attached to or responsible for the well-being of the project. This often led to neglect or outright destruction of the new building or school after the NGO departed. Hence, the citizens of Golem initially hoped for some of this "easy" money and hoped that we would do everything for them to get it.

We worked hard to help the community of Golem overcome these issues. However, the first thing we had to do was examine our own beliefs and attitudes about the project in order to help. We needed to learn more about the area of Golem and its history and culture. We could not assume they were the same as all other villages in Albania where we had worked. Just as there are cultural and regional differences across the United States, so there are differences across Albania.

We also had to be careful not to be judgmental. They were not ignorant or backward, but never had the opportunity to strategize or problem-solve on such a macro-level. We needed to treat them with respect as we would anyone else. This was clear both for me as an American and for my staff as Albanians. It was difficult for me not to react poorly to Golem's lack of problem-solving skills. In America, problem-solving skills are taught to young children and are built into the curriculum of middle and high schools. I had to realize that the people of Golem, while they did not possess those certain skills, had a myriad of other skills (such as basic survival skills and knowing how do a lot with a little) that would serve them well in their attempts to solve their community problems.

For the Albanian staff, we had to deal with some prejudice against "villagers." In Albania, there is a huge difference in the quality of city life compared to life in the country. The rural areas of Albania are mostly farmland, mostly subsistence-level survival, and the education opportunities are very limited. Most city dwellers in Albania consider non-city dwellers as "backward" and "ignorant." The staff had to confront their own prejudices against country people and create new lenses in which to see them.

We addressed this lack of problem-solving skills with training. First, we trained our staff how to strategize and problem-solve and they, in turn, taught the community group, who (we hoped) would, in turn, teach the rest of the community. Although this extra training slowed down the time line of our project, it was essential to its success. After the training, the community workers spent a lot of time walking the community group through the process and answering endless questions. It was interesting to watch the group progress in the development of these skills. It was at the end of the project, during the evaluation process, when the group labeled themselves as having a "practical sense of problem-solving."

Addressing the problem of little follow-through was more difficult. We continuously stressed the importance of actually doing what you say you will do. The staff and I were often frustrated with coming to the village for a meeting and finding out that the duties they assigned to themselves the previous week were unfinished or, at best, finished poorly. The most critical aspect of this issue involved attendance at local Commune council meetings. The Commune council meetings occur once a month when the elected village leaders meet to discuss community issues, decide on policy, and allocate community funds. All citizens are entitled by law to attend these meetings and speak at the end. This should have been the easiest and most direct way for citizens to communicate with their elected representatives and have an impact on decision making.

However, no citizens ever went to these meetings. (I had a hard time getting my staff to attend their own council meetings in their respective neighborhoods.) Certainly, these meetings can be boring and, in truth, many leaders did not want citizens to attend. If citizens attended, then the meeting's agenda was transparent and the leaders would be held accountable for their actions. Citizen attendance in Golem at these meetings was usually zero. Our field coordinators pushed their citizens to attend these meetings. In the beginning, everyone agreed to attend, but never did.

A few members finally did attend and realized what a perfect opportunity it was for them to speak to their leaders, raise awareness about the water problem issue, and ask for action. When the rest of the members realized this opportunity, they also attended and used the setting of the Commune council meeting as an avenue to resolve their issues. Once the members realized the importance of following through on what they said they would do and that it was important for every member to "pull his or her weight," progress quickly ensued and the group moved toward their goal much more quickly.

We did not successfully address the "do it for me" attitude. We frequently tried to explain to the group that they needed to act on their own behalf. Our project was not a permanent project and our final goal was to leave the group with enough community development skills to solve other community problems on their own, after our exit from Golem. We tried to explain how important it was that they learn for themselves how to organize and advocate on current and future issues. We never transformed the "do it for me" attitude into a "we can do it ourselves" attitude.

We made progress but never achieved this goal. Although this lack of initiative cost much time and caused many headaches, the group did eventually enjoy some level of success with their bigger activities and duties.

Questions

Now that the author has presented information about the formation of the citizens group and the cultural barriers they faced, its time to begin planning for action. Therefore, answer the following questions.

1. First, explore the literature about community practice and various community organization methods and locate Rothman's three types of community action (Rothman & Tropman, 1995). What category of community action does this project best fit? Please explain your answer.

2. As you prepare for action, and based on the category of community practice discussed above, what steps must you take as the organizer to initiate action toward solving the potable water problem in Golem?

3. What role will you play as the organizer? Please explain your role and position in this effort.

4. Develop a written plan of action based on the information provided by the author, the professional community practice literature, and your experiences as a social worker. Engage classmates and/or colleagues in a dialogue about the best ways to approach intervention in this case. What significant barriers remain that could block progress toward goal achievement?

Taking Action

We found that the community development process, from engagement to implementation and evaluation was a process of compromise and negotiation. The decision to work on potable drinking water in the village was easy for the group. Because nobody had water in his or her home, it was an urgent problem that affected everyone and the benefits would be clear if successful. The planning stage was not so difficult either, but the action stage proved most difficult.

Once the "issue" was decided upon, the citizens of Golem spent several meetings creating their action plan. They concretized their vision: "Golemi me uje te pijshem," which means, "Golem with drinking water." Our job was to help them create their plan, with problem solving through mediation, but not to help implement the solution—that was the job of the citizens group. The process of creating the plan was a mixture of problem solving, strengths-based assessment, and use of the "miracle question" as in solution-focused therapy (Berg, 1995). The citizens responded well to this approach. For example, questions such as, "If you woke up tomorrow and a miracle happened overnight, what would be different?" stimulated intense conversation and led to a vision, which ultimately led the citizens to a concrete plan of action.

We helped create a road map detailing the project in terms of who, what, where, when, and why. That is, every member of the group had a job to do and a deadline by which to do it. The group made decisions through consensus and, if consensus was not possible, by voting. The goal of the plan was to get the Commune office to agree to fund a water system for Golem. A new system was best, but fixing the original pipes and pumps was acceptable.

Methods: Strengths-Based Approach

There are many ways to approach community organizing. In Albania, we used many existing methods and, out of necessity, also developed our own methods of working in the poor villages of rural Albania. Most of the established community practice methods are based on American or Western European values and communities and did not directly apply in rural Albania. Because of cultural differences, we learned about the necessity of considering the Albanian people, history, and culture in our work if we hoped to succeed (Johnson, 1999). Ultimately, we developed an approach that combined a strengths-based (Glicken, 2004) and solution-focused approach (Berg, 1995) to reach our goals.

Our first task was to discover the resources and assets within the community (Kretzmann & McKnight, 1993; Scales & Streeter, 2004). We needed to learn their strengths to make use of them in this project. The field coordinators, together with the core group, created a community map. Taking large flip chart paper, we drew a map of Golem, drawing in all the resources: the Commune office, the schools, small businesses, and health center. Looking at our picture was in actuality a bit discouraging since Golem did not possess many resources. The participants became discouraged until they stumbled upon Golem's greatest resource: the people of Golem. Once the group added the people to their map, the participants realized that they did have strength and that maybe they could reach their goal.

As a group we discussed how best to mobilize these resources. Remember, this was the first time that citizens saw themselves as "resources." We planned to recruit as many citizens as possible. Although local media was nonexistent, we also planned to use the media in the capital and, if possible, national media—television, radio, and print media—to pressure elected officials and convince local authorities to become allies. We also needed the officials to help the citizens group convince the Commune to fund the project.

Adapting the "Miracle Question" to Community Organizing

As we strategized, planned, implemented, and built support, we discovered that the "miracle question" (Berg, 1995) worked well in helping citizens envision a better future. Our staff asked this question of the citizens group, who in turn asked their neighbors and other community members an Albanian version of the miracle question: "If you woke up tomorrow, and your life was better, and your community was better, what would it look like?" This question made it easy to plan an intervention and easy to convince people to work with us, because they could quickly say, "tomorrow my village would have no trash" or, in Golem, "tomorrow I would turn on my kitchen faucet and water would come out and I wouldn't have to walk two kilometers to get water."

I never used the miracle question in my community practice in America and had not planned to use it in Albania, but we were having a difficult time getting the group to think long-term and vision a final goal. During a conversation with the staff, I decided to ask the staff the miracle question. They responded so well with a discussion around the question itself that I decided to use it in the field—to adapt this idea from individual and family therapy at the micro-level to community organizing at the mezzo- and macro-level.

Taking Action

The first step in our plan was to recruit more citizens willing to work toward getting water in Golem. The group accomplished this by going from home to home and talking to citizens. What they discovered was that many citizens were "suspicious" of the success of the project and refused to help or give their support. Therefore, we called a community meeting to discuss the issue. The local authorities who were our allies, members of the core group, and our two field coordinators presented the project and why the project needed broader community support. Eighty citizens attended this meeting, increasing the overall number of participants to the project to 150.

The next step was to help the community decision makers become aware of the urgency of the problem and make them realize that the citizens were organizing to solve this problem and would not take no for an answer. The group circulated a petition for Golemites to sign, stating their support for the project. The petition was given to the Commune council to ask for (or demand) their support. Two hundred people signed the petition before presenting it to the council at the next Commune council meeting. Surprisingly, the Commune council accepted the petition and agreed to fix the water pipes. The few citizens that presented the petition at the meeting were happy and reported their success at the next community group meeting.

Unfortunately, this was not the end of the process. The next week, a few members of the core group met with their local authorities to follow up on the Commune council's decision. The council told the group that although the Commune supported their efforts, the Commune had no money to fix even one pipe, let alone the whole village's water system. The council then asked the group to leave. Group members reported this event at the next community meeting and the entire group became discouraged. We decided to regroup and restrategize. Our first plan was not successful, so we asked the group to create a new plan that would bring us closer to our goal.

Turning up the "Heat" on the Commune Council

Alinsky (1972) believed that community action must occur in stages. That is, organizations should continually pressure decision makers through a series of increasing public expression and pressure as the decision makers fail to respond. First, the group tried quiet negotiating. While it seemed that this tactic was successful, the Commune council changed its decision about support for the water project. Hence, the next step was to increase the pressure on the council to act.

The group developed new tactics. First, they circulated a new petition, obtained more signatures, and send it to the radio station in the next village to read on the air during the news. They also sent it to the national TV station hoping they would mention it on the news as well. Second, they sent as many people as they could gather to the next Commune council meeting in order to put pressure on the council and show their strength and solidarity. Lastly, after accomplishing the first two tactics, the group invited the Commune council and local authorities to a town meeting with citizens to discuss the water issue in Golem. The group also invited the media.

The new petition generated more signatures than the first. The group sent it to radio stations, Albania's national television station, and the Albanian Central Authority. Twenty citizens attended the next Commune council meeting and addressed the council about their problem and possible solutions. In July 2002, four months after they began, the group held a community meeting with local officials, citizens, and the media.

Questions

The author described several common issues facing any grassroots action, wherever these actions occur. That is, often decision makers will make a temporary decision to support a community group in an effort to quiet the group, and not necessarily fix the problem. Decision makers can later change the decision after the group has quieted or disbanded. A community organizer's task is often maintaining group cohesion and motivation to keep the pressure on decision makers until a solution is completed. Saul Alinsky (1972) speaks to this dynamic exceptionally well. While his writing was generated in the 1960s, his ideas and tactics remain relevant today.

1. Study Alinsky's (1972) community organizing theory and tactics. Develop a short summary that describes his ideas and how to mobilize grassroots groups in a change effort.

2. Alinsky has specific ideas about how to approach institutional decision makers, where and how change occurs, and when it is appropriate to take community action public in an effort to pressure decision makers to change. Include in your review a detailed understanding of his ideas about this issue.

Based on his work, was the group in Golem appropriate to go public with their issue at this time? Please defend your answer.

3. **Based on his work and the information provided in this chapter, what strategies would you use to keep the group motivated and the pressure on local authorities?**

4. **If this strategy did not work, what is your plan of action for the next "round" of effort? How would you keep the pressure on the Commune council if they did not respond favorably in the community meeting, with the media present?**

A Solution

During the meeting, everyone (including the Commune council) agreed on a solution. Since a new water system would cost tens of thousands of dollars and fixing the old one would cost only slightly less, they reached a compromise. The Commune council agreed to put rehabilitating the water system of Golem into the Commune budget for the next year. In the meantime, the Commune would pay to have freshwater trucked into Golem two times per week from the reservoir. The group agreed to this compromise solution and was happy with their efforts.

Two weeks later, the first truck rumbled into the center of Golem and its citizens happily queued up to fill their empty jugs with freshwater. The community group, happy with their victory, decided to meet again to find another community issue that they could work toward solving. Upon the completion of their first project, the group stated, "Kur organizohemi se bashku dhe angazhohemi behemi me te fuqishem per te zgjidhur problemet e komunitetit," which means, "When we organize ourselves together we become powerful to solve community problems."

Ethical Issues

The ethical issues that arose while working in the village of Golem were of two types; issues the community and staff faced when working with the village of Golem. We dealt with both issues through open dialogue and democratic decision-making.

First, the community had to face how to handle villagers that refused to support the project but would benefit from its success. This issue divided the group. If they were successful in their bid for water in Golem, all of the homes would have running water. However, some members of the group believed the dissidents in the village should have their water turned off. These people based their beliefs on the idea that, "They aren't helping us, why should we help them?" and "They haven't worked hard (like we have) to get water, in fact, they are doing nothing and not even being supportive, so why do they deserve water?"

This became a divisive issue as people in the group began taking sides. It slowed the organizing and decision-making process. The field coordinators tried to solve this problem, to no avail. We brainstormed possible solutions to the problem and held a special meeting with the Golem group. We talked about the meaning and definition of community and the need to be inclusive in their definition of community. That is, communities are comprised of everyone, young and old, rich and poor, faithful and doubting. We then opened the meeting up to discussion, allowing all members to share their points of view. We encouraged the group to make a decision about this issue that day. They talked some more and could not agree. The group decided to put the issue to a vote. Everyone agreed to abide by the vote and move on. Fortunately (although by a slim margin), the group voted to include the dissidents in the solution if they were successful.

Within our staff, the main issue we faced dealt with balancing the hopes and growing confidence of the group with the hard face of reality. While we wanted the Golem group to be confident in themselves as a community and to take risks, we also did not want to provide false hope or an overinflated sense of power. We knew from experience that solving water problems is difficult, because it requires money and substantial government support. The group in Golem had neither. We were ethically responsible not to make their lives worse. For example, most families in Golem owned a donkey or two that they used to haul water. What we did not want was for the citizens to sell their donkeys based on a promise of water from the government. This had happened in another community we worked in and the water never came. Soon, the people did not have water in their homes or donkeys to help haul water from the far off wells.

Similarly, we did not want to warn them against trusting the government, as that would create distrust and discourage people from taking action in the future. The group needed to learn this lesson on their own. However, we also believed that we needed to ensure that the group did not lose their livelihoods in the process. Hence, we needed to balance our role between being a "big brother" to the group and allowing them "feel their own feet," by making decisions on their own and dealing with the consequences. After all, we were trying to help them grow into an independent, competent community group that acted on its own volition. Groups must learn to act within the reality of their given circumstances. Sometimes, this means dealing with institutional decision makers that do not act in the people's best interest. This happens everywhere, not just in Albania.

Our staff spent a lot of time discussing this issue. Ultimately, we decided to warn the group not to sell their donkeys too soon, but to wait and make certain of having a permanent source of water in their homes. We told them the story of the other village and of their struggles. We used the experience of another village in Albania to help teach Golem. This turned out to be effective as the citizens of Golem appreciated the information and became more careful and wary of government promises made to them.

Questions

The citizen group in Golem had successfully negotiated a temporary solution to the water problem. While they did not achieve their ultimate goal, they had

arranged to have freshwater trucked into the village twice weekly. They also had a promise from the Commune council to place water system repairs in the next years' budget.

1. Based on your experience and reading of this case and the community practice literature, how would you judge the outcome of this case to this point? Was it a success or failure? Please explain your decision.

2. What next steps should the group take to ensure that this solution remains? What additional steps should the group take to ensure that the budgetary promises are fulfilled the following year?

3. When is the best time to terminate? That is, how do you judge when the local group is able to carry on without outside support? What indicators would you use to make this decision?

Termination

By the beginning of the next year, we were still working with the community group in Golem. We had not discussed as an organization when termination should occur. It soon became evident and increasingly urgent (budgetary constraints) to discuss when and how to terminate our project in Golem. The majority of the staff wanted to stay in Golem for the length of our funding. The Program Director agreed to discuss with the staff the importance of terminating our projects with community groups effectively for the well-being of our program and the community group. We discussed the reasons why we must stop working with community groups:

1. Limited resources and the need to reach as many communities as possible while our program still had funding.
2. Professional boundaries and not becoming so attached to each community to ensure their independence from our organization.
3. Local responsibility, meaning that at some point the communities needed to work on their own.

The staff decided that the appropriate time limit to work with one community group was through two cycles of issue solving. In Golem's case, the community workers could work with Golem through the process of solving one more community issue. The staff was trained to terminate the project, which involved talking about the end of the process while in the beginning phase so that everyone had clear expectations about how long the process would last. The field coordinators also reminded the group that they would not be able to collaborate with them on a permanent basis. Finally, staff was instructed to leave the door open to the community to reestablish contact if they need help or direction.

After project termination, we knew we could not cut off all contact with the groups immediately, so we coined a new phrase called "coffee groups." These groups had completed two cycles and were no longer meeting with us on a biweekly basis. The field coordinators would call up these groups about once a month to have a coffee to check in and see how things were going and if they needed any help.

We considered the project in Golem a success. In fact, the group of citizens in Golem accomplished more than most other projects. Yet, their success was tentative, since the Commune council had not approved funding for the following year. Moreover, since the Commune paid for the water trucks, they could decided to stop them at any moment. The citizens of Golem are a determined group and eager to test their newly learned community organizing skills by tackling another community issue. Their newfound success and a growing confidence in the power of community should serve them well in the future.

Questions

The author presented an interesting case. Taking a broad view of this case, reevaluate the author's work by responding to the following questions.

1. Take a moment to review the citizen group's progress. Based on the author's description, the professional literature, and the latest practice evidence, what occurred to account for the progress?

2. What was the theoretical approach or combination of approaches that appeared to work best?

3. Based on the work you have done earlier, what additional intervention(s) would you recommend? Use the literature and latest evidence to justify your recommendations.

4. Overall, what is your professional opinion of the work performed in this case? As always, refer to the professional literature, practice evidence, your experience, and the experience of student-colleagues when developing your opinion.

5. Based on this review, what additional or alternative approaches could have been used with this case? That is, if you were the practitioner, how would you have approached this case? Please explain and justify your approach.

6. As part of the termination process, what concerns would you express to the citizen group about the long-term effects of the process they have been through? What supports could you offer?

7. What did this case demonstrate that you could use in other practice settings. List the most important things you learned by studying this case and how you could use them in your practice career.

Bibliography _____

Alinsky, S. (1972). *Rules for radicals.* New York: Random House.

Berg, I. K. (1995). Solution-focused brief therapy with substance abusers, In A. M. Watson (ed.), *Psychotherapy and substance abuse: A practitioner's handbook* (pp. 223–242). New York: Guilford Press.

Glicken, M. D. (2004). *Using the strengths perspective in social work practice.* Boston: Allyn and Bacon.

Johnson, J. L. (1999). *Crossing borders—Confronting history: Intercultural adjustment in a post-Cold War world.* Lanham, MD: University Press of America.

Kretzmann, J. P., & McKnight, J. L. (1993). *Building communities from the inside out: A path toward finding and mobilizing a community's assets.* Chicago: ACTA Publications.

Rothman, J., & Tropman, J. E. (1995). *Strategies of community intervention* (5th ed.). Itasca, IL: F. E. Peacock.

Scales, T. L., & Streeter, C. L. (2004). Introduction: Asset building to sustain rural communities. In T. L. Scales & C. L. Streeter (eds.), *Rural social work: Building and sustaining community assets* (pp. 1–6). Pacific Grove, CA: Brooks/Cole.

3

Mothers vs. The Board of Education

Kimberly S. Crawford &
Jerry L. Johnson

I was born an eight-pound, nine-ounce, bald social worker. This is how my family would laughingly describe me. However, I suppose I could not argue with their characterization entirely. I raised my family, before returning to school and entering professional social work. I have, however, been involved in political and community social work service for more decades than I can, or will, admit. I have a long and varied history of inserting myself into calls for justice for communities within the United States and abroad. The case I outline for you here hits much closer to home. Suddenly, I found myself not seeking social justice for the disenfranchised "out there" in some anonymous or unfamiliar community, but at home. This was my neighborhood.

The intent of the case is to highlight a community of neighbors that worked together and learned to utilize the resources available to them to achieve their own social justice. Initially, they felt powerless to act against a larger system of power and authority. They became virtual prisoners within their own community to the will of the newest, most powerful resident. When they asked to be heard, they were ignored. When they sought assistance from the city's public officials, they received a lukewarm reception accompanied by inaction. Over a nine-month period, this community learned to organize its efforts, and effectively make changes in pursuit of justice.

Where Am I?

When working in community service, I feel it is necessary to have a real understanding of the community I am serving. This understanding should go beyond the demographics readily available on the Internet. The more enveloped you can

49

become in the community, the more affective you can be in its service. Consider a community's history, its current flavor, and situation that have called you into service, as well as its future goals and aspirations. Look at the past, present, and future of the community from multiple lenses. From each of these perspectives, consider who makes up the community and the surrounding systems that support and affect its residents.

Let me familiarize you with this neighborhood. This particular neighborhood borders a recently revitalized historical district. It sits adjacent to the downtown community of one of the larger metropolitan areas in Michigan. Many of the homes are of grand scale. It would not be unheard of to find dumbwaiters, woodwork of fine artisanship, and even a full ballroom within the homes of this area. These were grand homes that reflected Michigan during its industrial boom.

However, this neighborhood has long since housed the elite. It no longer reflects excesses, but a community that is surviving. The community is abundant with young working-class families and young dual-income couples of modest means. The houses now reflect the struggle present in the community. The market value of the once prized homes has experienced notable decline. A four bedroom, four bathrooms home is now readily available for approximately $93,000.

Nestled within the community had once been a thriving college campus. The business college grew to university status, outgrowing this site, which was land-locked within the neighborhood. It became necessary to vacate the buildings and relocate. The city's public school district gradually began to inherit and occupy the buildings. One particular building on a corner lot remained unoccupied. This building was constructed in 1924. It quickly began to show its years without upkeep. The building deteriorated, becoming a community eyesore. Abandoned buildings add more than cosmetics to a neighborhood. They can reflect on a community's spirit, as well as a projected state of apathy by the residents, as seen by those outside the community.

Abandoned buildings are regular targets for urban crime. According to Wilson and Kelling's (1982) "broken window syndrome," abandoned properties send a signal to criminals about the apathetic concern a community and policy makers place on a property. This exacerbates the crimes of graffiti, loitering, and destruction of property present at these sites. After four years, serving as the target of vandalism and home to misdemeanor crimes, the public school system acquired the building.

Questions

1. The author speaks about the benefits of immersion in the communities that you serve. A particular emphasis is placed on researching the historical events of the community. It is important to place that information in context with the current situation of concern. Once you have established that foundation, you can more thoroughly address the community's current goals to recti-

fy their situation. Assume for a moment, that you were asked to address the concerns of a community with which you are unfamiliar.

2. What measures would you take to garner a better understanding of, and therefore better serve, this community? Remember to attend to the community's past, present climate, and future goals.

I Have Always Wanted to Have a Neighbor, Just Like You. –Fred Rogers

The community breathed a collective sigh of relief. They had a new neighbor; one who could share in the pride of their community. The neighborhood quickly organized a group of representatives to welcome the administrative staff from the local school district into their new home. This task force organized a meeting, inviting community members, future staff of the newly acquired building, the district superintendent, and the president of the school board. The intent of the meeting was to build a relationship with its newest resident. The neighborhood wanted to welcome and offer its support and input to the representatives about to inhabit the once abandoned building.

The presentations and casseroles were dutifully prepared. The residents came to greet representatives from the school district en masse. Not a single invited guest from the school district chose to attend. This was a slap in the face to the residents, who had gone out of their way to arrange the event. It was a blatant sign of disrespect. It was ironically symbolic of the relationship that was about to unfold.

Beauty Has Its Price

Over the next several months, the neighbors began to see life in the once desolate building. There was a virtual parade of utility trucks on a daily basis. Painters, plumbers, electricians, carpenters, and city inspectors all brought new life to the once crumbling monstrosity. You could literally see the spirits rise in unison with the restoration process. The Fourth of July block party brought with it the first stirrings of discontent. As residents began to discuss their joy over the beautification process, they began to collectively discuss the inconvenience the workers' trucks were causing. They looked with foresight at the potential parking dilemma when a full staff inhabited the building.

The community saw a need to address their concerns with the district superintendent. This was an older neighborhood. Many houses did not have garages, or even driveways. This forced most residents to park on the street. It had long since been an accepted practice that the parking space located directly in front of the home "belonged" to the residents of that home. It was discourteous to use the space in front of a neighbor's home. Before the school year brought a greater parking problem to the area, the parking situation needed attention. The neighborhood developed a task force to speak with the president of the school board.

Who Will Step Forward?

The task force consisted of five women from the two blocks bordering the building's corner lot. These women did not share a history of empowerment. It was significant that these five women stepped up to take the lead in this effort. Their lives reflected the series of oppressive systems involved in their lives. Therefore, it was noteworthy to consider the growth in their perceptions of strength when they took on this effort and saw it through its ultimate outcome. Let's take a moment to consider the personal history these women brought with them to the present.

None of these women had held a position of employment or in the community outside of their home in the years that they had been married. The needs of their families consumed their lives. They all hailed from, and have assumed their role, in patriarchal households. Four of these women were in their late twenties, early thirties. The fifth was in her mid fifties. Before they formed this task force, they had no real experience organizing an effort more involved than the annual potluck Fourth of July block party.

What part might culture have played in their experience with oppression? It is definitely a confound that must be considered whenever you are working with clients of diversity. It plays a role whether your client is from the dominant culture or that of a minority. These five women represented diverse backgrounds.

The eldest, Gretchen, is a German American. She met her husband, a retired Sgt. Major, when he was a Corporal serving in the 411th Military Police Company. He was on a six-week Reforger exercise rotation. She was a housekeeper in the hotel where he spent his leave. They were married within two months of their meeting. They had been married for thirty-three years, and raised four sons. Gretchen lost both parents as a teenager. She had not returned to Germany and had no contact with anyone from her homeland.

Mary-Clare is of Irish American heritage. She was raised a Catholic but converted to Christian Reformed when she met and married her husband. She had never lived outside of the city limits. Her parents remained in the house where she grew up. Three of her five siblings still live in the vicinity, but she had no contact with her family. Mary-Clare became pregnant with her first child in her junior year of high school. Her family admonished her for the "shame she had brought to the family." She married the 26-year-old father of her child. They have been married for seven years and added two additional children to their family.

Lisa laughingly described herself as a "mutt," not exactly a positive description for someone who can claim a varied cultural background. Lisa claimed that her family never espoused to any particular lineage. She recalled them regularly proclaiming, "You are a proud American. That is all that matters." Lisa married her first and only boyfriend. She and her high school sweetheart were married one month after their graduation. Her husband went to work on the line in the factory in which his father and older brother worked, and his grandfather retired. Lisa and her husband have two children.

Rae is an African American. Rae grew up in a predominantly African American community in the center city. She met her husband at the local university, while working as a cashier in the bookstore. He was completing his undergraduate degree in elementary education. They dated for eleven months before he proposed. They were married two months after his graduation. They have one child. Both Rae and her husband are close to their families and extended families. They have prepared an extra room for Rae's grandmother, who will be moving in with them shortly.

Seleta is Mexican American. Both sets of her grandparents were first generation Mexican American. Seleta's family honored their heritage. Her family tradition honored their cultural traditions. She married a man ten years her senior. He is also Mexican American and had been included in traditional family activities until Seleta was 18 years old. On her eighteenth birthday, he proposed marriage to Seleta. They were married six months later. Her husband is an electrician in business with her second cousin. They have been married three years and have one daughter.

Religion was a central focus in the choices these women made in their lives. Religiosity can play a part in what a woman and her community perceives as her "role" in her family and her immediate environment. Of the five women in question, three considered themselves Calvinists. The remaining two were members of the United Christian Reformed Church, located just one block from their homes. Both of these religious sects hail from fundamentalist principles.

All five husbands were active members of the Promise Keepers organization. This was an organization established by fundamentalist Christian men. The Promise Keepers believe that the Bible annoints the male as the head of his household. It is his responsibility to lead and protect his family. Among fundamentalist Christian evangelicals, 90 percent affirm the biblical injunction of male leadership in the family (Maton, 1989). These women appeared to hold true to these principles in every aspect of their lives. It was their practice to serve males within their systems. It was foreign for them to question male authority. It was interesting to watch as this questioning of male authority began to emerge as they addressed their concerns over the parking situation with the school district.

These women accepted a power differential based on gender. The culture within their environment had supported dependence, submission, and self-sacrificing behaviors. The culture these women emerged from did not urge them to seek out social justice. This was not their role. They did not feel capable of affecting change. Moreover, it was "not their place" to question the decisions enacted by male figures of authority. This brings to mind a sentiment expressed by Miriam Polster as she discussed what it involved to grow up female in our Western society, "(it) leaves a physical residue that cripples and deforms all but the most exceptional women" (as cited in Franks & Burtle, 1974). To create such "exceptional" women, appropriate supports must be in place to support their individual strengths. At the time these five women first tackled this effort, they had no experience with these supports. They did not fully recognize their strengths.

Gretchen, the eldest of the women, assumed the lead role in organizing their efforts. She had been a prior military spouse and had twenty years of experience working with other women in military wives' support groups. Over the years, she hosted teas for the wives and reenlistment receptions for the husbands. She organized countless bake sales and activities to honor and support her husband and his fellow soldiers. She had never advocated for her own needs. Nevertheless, she was the most qualified among the five to lead the cause.

They met around her kitchen table that morning in July. It took two full pots of Folgers decaffeinated coffee and almost an entire batch of Tollhouse cookies before they rallied their strength to call the office of the school board president. Their intent was to make him aware of the potential parking dilemma they foresaw for the staff in the fall. At this point, they felt it was imperative to come to a resolution, without coming across offensively. They wanted it to be a "nice" meeting. The meeting was set for the end of the week.

Questions

1. The five women on the neighborhood task force represent the pluralism in the community. They represent diverse ages, races, and ethnicities. Clearly, this is not a case where one particular age group, race, or ethnicity is subjected to discrimination. Why are these factors significant to this case? What does the age, race, or ethnicity of these women potentially represent in terms of their unique strengths and challenges? Discuss why the age, race, and ethnicity of a client are always a factor worthy of consideration, whether the client is of the majority or minority population.

2. Religiosity is an additional component that has the potential to affect a client's values in the realm of social justice. It can also play a role in the client's ability or willingness to step forward and pursue his or her cause. As you continue the reading, site at least two examples where religion might have been a factor in the steps these women chose to take. How might their actions be reflected on their religious principles?

3. The individuals from the public school system all hold graduate and postgraduate degrees. Additionally, their employment consists of positions of authority and responsibility. Conversely, the five-woman task force hold high school diplomas, or GED equivalencies. They have not held positions in the workforce since they were married. Jobs held before they were married were low-wage hourly positions. Education and the positions of opportunity they afford represent an obvious power differential between these two positions. What measures would you take to help minimize this obstacle?

Do You Always Catch More Flies with Honey?

When you look at the goals and tactics this group of women intended to employ, it was easy to identify the effects of living within an oppressive culture had placed on their lives. These women appeared inhibited by the traditional roles expected of them as women within their society. Corey and Corey (1997) outline five culturally accepted stereotypes placed on women in our society. These same five stereotypes seemed to be limiting the women in our group. According to Corey and Corey (1997), women who exhibit an independent spirit are often viewed as hostile and aggressive. Rather than being rational and logical, women are expected to act with emotion. Women are often content to form relationships, rather than striving ahead to achieve their goals. Those women who exhibit behaviors that are not home-oriented, submissive, and indecisive are considered unfeminine. It is also considered a woman's "nature" to be caring, nurturing, and kind. However, they do not necessarily expect these qualities to be returned to them in their interactions.

The women on the task force seemed to adhere to these stereotypical behaviors of submission. They approached their potential adversary from a place of contrition. They wanted to "share" their concerns with the school board president. It was important to them that they not appear aggressive or offensive. They wanted to bring about a positive working relationship with this male-dominant authority. They wanted to be perceived as "nice" people.

Question

Recall the factors of race, gender, religiosity, and education that we discussed previously. Do you believe those factors had a role in this first encounter? List at least three examples where these factors should be considered. What steps could you take to meet these challenges?

A First Glimpse at Success

When this group of women arrived at their appointment with the president of the school board, his administrative assistant asked them to wait in the outer office. After waiting ten minutes, they were told that there would be a change in plans. The school board president was unavailable to meet with the task force on the day of the appointment. However, the superintendent had agreed to see them. The women did not come armed with a written copy of their concerns, or a proposal for change. They spoke informally about their concerns about the impending parking problem. They did not want to appear too aggressive. They opted to leave their notebook at home. They wanted the meeting to be conversational and friendly.

The superintendent allowed them sufficient time to express themselves and vowed to entertain their concerns. He recognized that the building did not house an adjacent parking lot. Parking in the upcoming school year would present a predicament for the incoming staff as well as the residents of the surrounding area if an alternative could not be found. He claimed to be intent on finding such an alternative. At the close of the meeting, he asked them to leave their names, addresses, and phone numbers with his administrative assistant and he would get back to them with a decision.

The superintendent brought the concerns to the president of the school board. They agreed that this matter needed to be addressed before the full school board. After bringing these concerns to their attention, monies were made available to rent two church parking lots in the near vicinity. These parking lots were large enough to house the full staff and any visitors to the facility. They were located one block from the premises. Prior to the school term, each staff member would receive a parking sticker, designating their eligibility to access these lots. The lots would be patrolled. Anyone without an appropriate sticker would be ticketed. The sticker served to keep residents from using the lots as overflow parking and ensure parking availability for the staff.

The superintendent's administrative assistant called a representative from the task force. The information to rent the lots for the staff to address the neighborhood's concern for available parking was relayed. A follow-up letter was sent to each of the group members, detailing the decision of the board. It included a map of the neighborhood, complete with a description of the parking lots. The mailing also included a letter from the president of the school board thanking the committee for bringing this concern to their attention.

The community was satisfied. They had voiced their concerns, and they were heard. Their actions had resulted in a positive outcome. A sense of empowerment spread throughout the community. They once again could look at the newly restored, three-story brick building with a sense of hopefulness. This group of neighbors had built on the strengths they possessed to advocate for change. They brought foresight, and knowledge of the community requirements. They directed their collective concerns to an individual who had the authority to address and make the changes necessary a reality. Their actions had brought about the positive change they had been seeking. There was a real sense of accomplishment. This accomplishment would later foster the empowerment these women would need to continue to seek justice for their community.

Questions

The neighborhood task force achieved a positive result from their encounter with the school district representative. They presented their case in a format in which they were comfortable. The school district responded positively. They rectified the potential parking dilemma for the neighborhood residents by providing offsite parking for their employees.

1. **What strengths were they able to bring to the negotiation?**

2. What challenges could you foresee, from this initial contact, if further negotiations become necessary?

3. How might you have advised this group of women?

What Happened to the Success We Gained?

August brought the beginning of the school year. Staff began to filter into their new place of employment. Residents were disappointed to see their parking spaces occupied by the new staff members. It was plausible that the staff had not been made aware of the parking arrangements set forth by the school board. After all, they were still moving their personal effects into their new workspace. Calls were made to the administrators of the new occupants. While they were readily unavailable, the appropriate administrative assistants documented their messages. The calls went unanswered. The parking quandary continued.

Several months passed with the problem unresolved. Calls were made repeatedly to the building requesting that the parking lots rented by the district be utilized. The requests were ignored. Often residents found the space in front of their homes occupied when they returned home. They were forced to park several blocks from their homes, with their children or groceries in tow. Without an employee sticker, they were unable to utilize the church parking lots for fear of receiving a parking violation. Two neighbors had used the parking lot after returning home and not having access to the space in front of their homes. They each received $20 citations. In response, neighbors began spending their early morning hours watching the parking spaces in front of their homes. To the outsider, this behavior may have seemed excessive, even ridiculous. From within, it was a matter of necessity.

This had become more than an inconvenience. It was a growing matter of disrespect. Administrators of the building had not gone so far as to acknowledged their concerns. Neighbors believed that if they spoke with the owners of these vehicles face-to-face, they would achieve the results they were seeking. It was inconceivable that someone would meet them, listen to their concerns, and not adhere to their wishes. Some residents chose to place notes on the windshields of vehicles, requesting that they park in the parking lots provided. Others chose to go outside and meet with the employees when they parked their vehicle in front of their home, or when they returned to retrieve it at the end of the workday. Their requests, whether written or personally delivered were ignored.

The patterns continued. The community was beginning to feel helpless. They had attempted to voice their concerns with the president of the school board and the district's superintendent. They had shared their views with the administrators on the premises and the employees directly. All these efforts appeared fruitless. No changes had been accomplished. The employees still refused to relinquish the convenience of parking on the street in front of the building, rather than the lots provided one block away. Michigan's winter weather had ascended on the community, which exacerbated the conditions. When the parking spaces on the street were full, employees began parking in, or across the driveways of the homes adjacent to their building. Residents were often forced to park several blocks away and hike in the snow and ice to reach their homes.

Question

Consider the levels of oppression these women have experienced throughout their lives. Now, let's put that in context with the measures that they have taken to make the school district and its employees accountable for their actions and inactions. Given these experiences, how would you characterize their reaction to the noncompliance by the school district?

Is There Another Way?

The community felt that they had exhausted their options with the school district and its personnel. They approached the city for help. They asked the city to post parking restrictions on the street. They further requested that police be made available to enforce both the proposed parking restrictions and the current violations of parking in, or blocking private drives. The city informed the residents that their request would be submitted for review. A promise was made to increase available patrols in the area to enforce the current parking violations. The community had once again voiced their concerns to an individual in power. This individual had the authority to make the changes requested. Promises had once again been made to address their concerns. Unfortunately, these commitments did not come to fruition. Their concerns were once again disregarded.

The families had attempted to come to an understanding with the occupants of the building, to no avail. After months of noncompliance, they felt compelled to involve the city. They requested help enforcing the existing parking laws to keep their driveways clear of unwanted vehicles. Their pleas were once again disregarded. They saw only inaction of their requests. The community had spent months repeatedly advocating for a positive change. No one appeared to be listening. No one appeared to place value on this community, or its concerns. They had earned a reasonable response of helplessness.

Question

This neighborhood task force made use of multiple venues to force the authorities to honor their agreement to solve the parking issue. Each of their attempts was thwarted. Take a moment to outline their experiences leading to learned helplessness. What measures would you take to support these women?

Consider the individual and collective strengths they have shown through this process. How could they be used to combat learned helplessness?

Welcome Home?

There were abundant sentiments of helplessness, but they were not hopeless. It was at this point that I returned to the community after working eight and a half months in the Republic of Panama. I pulled up to my home at 10:00 a.m. after an overnight, international flight. I counted four vehicles in my driveway, and one blocking the end of my driveway. It was an abrupt awakening to what my community had been experiencing in my absence. Within twenty-four hours, my kitchen was full and every coffee mug I owned was in some state of active use. We discussed our community's newest resident in graphic detail.

The residents who had been living with the experiences were exasperated. They spoke of their frustrations and the attempts they had made to bring about justice to their situation. One story led to the next. Oftentimes the stories appeared to overlap as they began to talk more hurriedly over the top of each other's story. If you drew back from the words and became cognizant only of the pace and the passion, you could almost feel the pitch of the fever. This room was alive with their common cause. They were engrossed in their frustration of injustice.

Maybe this was more than a group of neighbors welcoming me home. These were my neighbors. They knew me. They knew my history. They understood my passion for my work. Maybe this was one more attempt to seek advice, to gain another partner in their pursuit of justice. I listened to their cause and the measures they had taken to advocate for change. I applauded their efforts. I needed them to feel heard. I needed to share with them the respect I held for the stance they had undertaken for all of us. In the end, I also felt it was necessary to consider the positive effects of having an occupant in the once vacant and dilapidated building. Its occupancy and its renovation were positives that I thought needed to be considered.

Initially, the room became quiet. The silence did not remain in the room for long. Apparently, my neighbors realized that I had heard their concerns. I appreciated their efforts and was ready to partner with them to advocate for a positive result for the community. It was in recognizing this that they were able to also reflect on the benefits the occupancy had brought to the community. Once heard, this collection of neighbors was no longer defensive, but progressive thinkers.

Questions

1. It was important to allow the neighbors to be heard, before addressing the benefits of the building renovation. Why was it necessary to consider both the positives and the negatives of the newly renovated building and its inhabitants? How does this technique allow clients to move from "defensive" to "progressive thinkers?

2. As a social worker, it can be tempting to jump in and "fix" the problem. What are the benefits of stepping back in a more supportive role? Conversely, what is the negative impact of assuming a lead role to affect positive change in a community? Consider both of these positions from the perspective of the five-woman task force as well as the community.

Who Will Listen?

We were able to brainstorm about what had been and what could become effective measures to bring about positive change. The group of neighbors drew on their most recent history of success. They recalled achieving positive results when they first addressed the issue of parking with the president of the school board. The women thought that they could readdress their problem with the school board president and the superintendent and achieve similar positive results. The five female residents from the original task force organized themselves to speak with the officers of the school district. I had a working relationship with the school board president. It was agreed that the appointment would be made under my name. This time the president of the school board appeared to have time available on his calendar. An appointment was set with the president of the school board and the superintendent, within seventy-two hours.

I do not find it significant that I was able to garner an appointment with a man whom I had a previous working relationship. I do, however, believe it is notable to address this fact in the context of the five-woman task force from the neighborhood. This was a group of women who did not hold a college credit among them. Four of the five women were registered voters, but they had otherwise never involved themselves in political advocacy. As previously addressed, they hailed from an oppressive set of systems. Since the beginning of the school year, their pleas for justice had been reputed by the staff of the building, the president of the school board, the office of the superintendent, the city road commission, and the police department.

This group of women did not answer this experience by throwing up their hands in defeat. They had not asked me to take on this responsibility that they had been shouldering in my absence. Instead, they were able to use the knowledge and connections they had to take their next step forward. The women recognized the positive result they achieved through the superintendent's office the previous summer, when they had initially addressed their concerns regarding the parking. Their voices had been heard, and steps were activated to rectify the situation. They further understood the working relationship I had held with the president of the school board. They were able to affectively use this connection to link themselves to the office. Even after months of experiencing defeat, they remained committed to affecting change. More importantly, they had begun to believe that they held the power to take the measures necessary to bring about that change.

The meeting took place in the office of the superintendent. The school board president, the district superintendent, the president of the local teachers' union, the five-woman task force from the neighborhood, and I were all in attendance. We were seated at an oblong mahogany conference table. The two sides sat across from each other. At first glance, they appeared odd adversaries. Three middle-aged, white men, one in a navy suit the other two in khaki pants and navy sports coats, all reeking of Gray Flannel cologne, represented the school district. They were almost comical in their unified appearance. The neighborhood task force sat opposite these administrators. Their appearance was quite different. They were adorned in polyester stretch pants and matching $5 canvas tennis shoes purchased from the local discount store. The visual power differential was readily apparent.

The women began stating their case. Gretchen stated their purpose and began to read off in chronological sequence the attempts they had made to correct the issues in parking from a spiral notebook. The other four women read a short paragraph or two detailing their personal experience with the parking situation. The superintendent excused himself to take a phone call midway through this presentation. The task force waited while the superintendent completed his call and contacted his administrative assistant to make a follow-up appointment for the caller. The interruption lasted about three minutes. The significance of that interruption far exceeded the three minutes of time. The interruption was yet another example of the disrespect the school district had afforded this community. They may have been granted the opportunity for this meeting, but it was clear that the three officials did not intend to give credence to their cause.

The collective response from the district representatives was one of false helplessness. They claimed to understand the residents' concerns but were powerless to force their employees' hand. The president of the school board reiterated the fact that they had provided two parking areas in response to the request of the neighborhood. However, they did not have the authority to force their employees to utilize these lots. To add insult to injury, the president of the teacher's association added, "The employees will not be forced to use the lots located a block from the premises. It is more than simple inconvenience for them. Crime in this area is a concern to the staff. They did not feel safe walking to and from the parking lot. Most of them come from a different kind of area."

Question

The evidence in this case showed a habitual disregard for the community and their five-woman task force. Until this point, the disrespect has been behavioral. Now, a representative from the district verbally insulted them. His words questioned the worth of their community. When you look at this particular group of women, why would this have a more poignant impact? How can this negative experience be used as an empowerment tool?

The Strategy Changes

The tone of the meeting quickly took on a new flavor. These were no longer women pleading for mercy in a situation involving severe inconvenience to the residents.

This was their neighborhood. This was their home. This was a personal attack. These were now mothers defending the community in which they raise their families. Yes, Standard and Poor's rates the crime level in this district as a 4, compared with a national average of 3. If, in fact, there was a slightly elevated risk of crime in this area, why did the district consider the risk of safety to their employees paramount to that of the homeowners and their children? The school district devalued the residents of their surrounding community. It was difficult to imagine how this could have been more decisively portrayed.

There was a moment of stillness. I think we were all flabbergasted from what we had just heard. The shock lasted but an instant before the task force switched gears. It was no longer paramount to be perceived as "nice," or easy to work with. The parking situation these women had lived with through the months of exhaustive attempts took on a new value. They were not just fighting for resolution of the parking situation. Their position had repeatedly been ignored or devalued by the school system. The actions and inactions of those in position of power have been symbolic of the disrespect that has been afforded to the community members. Now, words had directly targeted the worth of their community.

The moment of shock had dissipated. The women looked to each other. Without a word, an agreement was made. As each of the women began to collect the paperwork they had spread out in front of them, Gretchen addressed their adversaries. She began by detailing the pattern of inaction the district had chosen to take. These were three men who held the authority to enforce the parking restrictions as they had outlined them. It was clearly their choice to ignore the needs of the community. They refused to take action that would force their employees to utilize the parking lots rented on their behalf. If they choose to continue this pattern of inaction, the community task force would be forced to take further action.

The meeting ended with a word of warning. The community did not want to bring embarrassment to their public school system. They told the officials sitting across from them that they would wait two weeks before taking further measures. Within those two weeks, these officials needed to take whatever measures necessary to enforce the parking guidelines drawn up by the school board the previous summer. If they chose inaction once again, the committee would be forced to bring embarrassment to the school district. This was the last word. The community task force thanked the men for their time, collected their things, and left the office.

Question

It was important to the five-woman neighborhood task force to appear "nice" in their first personal encounter with the school district. Now, these women were willing to demand justice in the matter. Take a moment to outline the events that have led these women from a position of oppression to one of empowerment. If you were working with these women, do you believe they have

reached the stage of empowerment, or was further work required? Please explain.

What Is Next?

This was about to become a very different ball game. We agreed to meet back in my kitchen within the hour. I grabbed Alinsky's *Rules for Radicals* (1972) off my book-shelves, returned the loving "words" of greeting from my cat, and began preparing nourishment for the women about to return to my kitchen. These women had grown exponentially through this process. They had addressed their concerns with the appropriate people in positions of authority for eight months. Coming to this point in the process was an amazing accomplishment. The outcome was still in the future, but they needed to be honored for the steps that they had taken. This was my intent when we sat down to our omelets. First, we needed to celebrate the strengths they had found and the measures that they had taken on behalf of themselves and their community. They saw an injustice and they have worked diligently to correct it. Yet, these women had their sights on more than a moral victory.

"Now what?" was the next sentiment. We needed to determine the next logi-cal step. It was equally important to decipher why this would be our chosen path. I shared a few passages from Saul Alinsky's *Rules for Radicals* (1972). Alinsky describes effective change as stemming first from revelation. Revolution should remain as a last resort. Effective communication, which should show respect for the values from both sides of the argument, is the first weapon in a successful battle. It is only after exhausting effective communication, without the onset of change, even incremental change, that an effort should precede to the next level. I wanted to point out to this group that they had indeed followed these steps outlined for successful organizers for social change.

Yes, in fact this would be a last ditch effort to bring about the change they had been advocating. They had exhausted their efforts to communicate with the people in positions of authority to bring about the justice they sought. Their cause was effectively dead. Regardless of the impact that it held for the community, and the energy they were willing to devote to it, the district and the city were unresponsive. It is only when all other tactics have been depleted that a cause should determine whether the end justifies it moving from a position of revelation to that of revolu-tion. These women needed to carefully consider this next step. It would involve practices utterly foreign to them.

There was no hesitation. These five women were ready to begin the next step in the process of bringing about the resolution to their problem. They began to brain-storm new ideas. Some of these ideas bordered on gruesome, some comical. There was sporadic laughter, raised voices, and occasionally cheers. This was a room empowered. They were filled with a renewed energy. They were ready for the next battle. They no longer resembled the five women I knew before they undertook this challenge. These women had a greater sense of the strengths they possessed. It is always a privileged to watch this growth process.

Once again, this group of women had the wherewithal to utilize the resources available to them. Whatever action they would eventually take, they knew it was necessary to involve the media. They had promised embarrassment would be the result of inaction, and they intended to be true to their word. They were well aware of my connection with the local NBC station. It was the leading news affiliate in the region, and they intended to use this relationship to link their actions to broad local market coverage. They further asked if they could use my name when contacting a local reporter whom I had worked with in the past. They recognized the resources that could be of service to their cause, and they took the necessary measures to use them to their benefit.

Question

This neighborhood task force attempted to inform and negotiate with the school district and the city road commission for eight months. Not every cause will move from discussion to action. Many times the parties will be able to negotiate a viable decision. When that doesn't occur, it is important to carefully weigh the decision to bring the cause to the next level. What is the significance of this move for this particular task force of women? What must one determine before utilizing public action to address your cause?

From Revelation to Revolution

If, in fact, this group was prepared to move from revelation to revolutionary tactics, it was important to keep several ethical considerations in mind. The next step in the strategic plan must be well thought out. Quick reactions are rarely, if ever, effective tactics. It is easy to fall prey to a spontaneous reaction when an individual or group with a passion for their cause feels defeated. It is imperative to take the time to plan an effective and appropriate response. An appropriate response is always goal-oriented. The chosen tactic should be designed to reflect the desired goal. Tactics must be chosen that would evoke a specific response. In this instance, the plan should clearly involve the parking spaces in question. The focus should not be on the school district or its personnel staffing the neighborhood building. The parking spaces must be the central issue, not the individuals involved.

As a social worker, I also felt that it was important to explain to them the Code of Ethics to which I adhere. I am bound by my professional code to do no harm. It is essential that nobody or nothing experience any degree of harm in our pursuit of justice. This leads back to our goal orientation. There should be no harm when our focus is rectifying the situation of our parking spaces. The target of our position remains the parking spaces, not an individual, group, or organization.

It was a lot to take in. We decided to meet again the following day. This would give everyone a chance to reflect on the steps they had taken and the alternatives for their future strategic plan. We were not looking for a "knee-jerk" reaction. Our next step would be well thought out, goal-oriented, and would have the potential of evoking the desired reaction. We would do no harm.

Question

The condescending words spoken by the school district representative had been harmful. The women in this neighborhood task force were hurt and angry, and rightfully so. The breakfast meeting allowed them an opportunity to vent their frustration in an environment where there was some commonality of emotion. It was important that they were able to express themselves openly and feel heard. Once they were provided this opportunity, it was necessary to determine an appropriate response.

According to the NASW Code of Ethics, it is essential to "do no harm" in the service of individual clients or communities. Before preceding, take a moment to review your Code of Ethics. Pay particular concern to the issue of harm reduction and community service. While adhering to your professional code, how would you address the concerns of this five-woman task force and your community?

One Last Attempt At Revelation, Brings a Plan

Before we reconvened, Rae had made one last attempt to contact the city commissioner's office. She inquired about the status of the street signs that had been placed "under advisement" four months earlier. She learned that the street signs they had requested restricting parking, were "in committee." There was no projected timetable for a decision. When Rae inquired as to what the commissioner's office expected the residents to do in the mean time, she was told that the community effectively had no recourse. Until a decision was made restricting parking, *any wheeled vehicle* had a legal right to occupy the parking spaces. He had just armed Rae with the information she needed to employ the next course of action.

When the task force reconvened, she shared this knowledge with the group. The plan was put into place. If the district did not enforce the parking guidelines, within the two weeks allotted, the task force would see that the parking spaces were unavailable to the staff members. When the employees returned to work the following day, every parking space would be filled "legally" with a wheeled vehicle. To make their position more poignant, it was decided that they would use bicycles, rather than motor vehicles. They set out to collect five hundred bicycles and tricycles for the two-block radius.

Question

I found it interesting that Rae made one more attempt to bring about a peaceful resolution to the situation before moving forward with action. Review Rae's background. What elements in Rae's past would lead her to take this additional step? Consider her experiences with oppression and empowerment. How did these experiences help her to sustain her belief in herself as a change-agent?

The Plan Takes on Life

Over the next week and a half, the residents busied themselves collecting bicycles and securing coverage from the media. One week before the demonstration was to take place, I contacted the office of the superintendent. I inquired as to whether he intended to take action on the parking situation in our community before the deadline imposed by the community members. His response was that his hands were tied. I believed that it was only fair for me to inform him that the task force was prepared to follow through with their response.

The two-week period between the meeting in the office of the superintendent and planned demonstration showed no movement from the school district. The staff of the building, however, was reactionary. Evidently, they had been informed of the meeting at the superintendent's office. They continued to park in the parking spaces, across and in the driveways of the residents. During the final two-week time frame, the staff members had become verbally offensive to the residents. They hollered back and forth to each other and regularly laid on their horns when they parked their cars in the morning and when they returned to them at the end of the workday. When they encountered one of the residents, they habitually raised their voices and spoke tersely to them.

The five-woman task force did not waver in their insistence of addressing the issue of the parking spaces, not the individuals involved. They busied themselves collecting bicycles. Every bicycle within the two-block radius would be utilized. Everyone within this area was asked to borrow bikes from family and friends to help fill the spaces. Still, the number of bicycles would fall far short of the spectacle required to make the statement they desired.

Again, the women met to discuss the dilemma they faced. We all discussed the means we had used to acquire the bikes already in our possession. I included the bikes I had been able to obtain from friends and colleagues outside of the local community. When I told the community's story, people wanted to help. I wanted them to understand that they belonged to more than just their locally based community. We all belong to what is referred to as "communities of identification" (Longes, 1990; Garvin & Tropman, 1992). These communities of identification represent some common feature the members hold. In addressing these communities of identification, we spoke of organizations and individuals that we share an identity.

Others in the group began to look at the avenues they possessed to acquire the large numbers of bikes they needed.

The two churches that the five women belonged to became the central focus of attention. They contacted their senior pastors for their help. The women were permitted to add an insert to the Sunday bulletin. The insert was used to explain the dilemma the neighborhood families had experienced and the steps they had taken to rectify the situation. They requested the help and prayers of their congregations.

Question

The five-woman task force was able to expand their base of support by employing their communities of identification. Take a moment to think about your communities of identification. If this scenario occurred in your community, what supports are available for you to activate? It can be an empowering exercise to identify the external strengths and supports available to you. How can you use this exercise in your practice? What clients would be most benefited by this exercise? Why?

Twenty-Four Hours to Go

Twenty-four hours before the demonstration, the task force went into action. Gretchen contacted the media to confirm their presence the following day. Rae, Lisa, and Mary-Clare busied themselves ensuring that a final count of bicycles was available to be moved in place the following morning. Seleta printed off a memo to the surrounding residents explaining their efforts. She asked their support in keeping this a silent demonstration. The display would have a greater voice if the community members remained silent. While the display was intact, no one was to address the staff members directly. This was another effort to ensure that no harm, including verbal harm, would come of their efforts.

On the evening before the event, bicycles seemed to be multiplying exponentially. Garages, backyards, and porches were jammed with bikes. The group had to hurry to create tags for the bikes, so they could be more easily identified and returned at the end of the event. Signs were made that would be placed throughout the collection of bicycles. They instructed nonresidents to use the parking lots provided for their needs.

A Silent Display Speaks Loudly

We met at 4:00 a.m. to begin parking the bicycles and tricycles in the designated parking spaces. By five o'clock other neighbors had joined our efforts. At the final count, there were 732 bikes and tricycles to be included in the display. The bikes were of every size, color, and condition imaginable. It was 6:00 a.m. before all the bicycles and signs were in place. Every parking space and driveway was awash with bicycles of every size, shape, and color. Neighbors were collected on porches and stoops across the two-block radius admiring the display. There was nothing to do but await the reaction.

The media was in place by 7:00 in the morning. We were able to make the first local news spot. The news media interviewed each member of the task force, and video of the event was played live. Our representatives were able to intimately describe the parking problem that had precipitated this event. Within the interviews, they outlined the efforts they had attempted over the eight-month period to rectify the situation. Regardless of the outcome, they had been given the opportunity to bring their cause in front of the public. In so doing, they were able to highlight the strengths they had explored throughout the process of advocating for their own justice.

When the staff began arriving for their workday, they were met with silence. While the neighbors recognized the vehicles as they drove past the now occupied parking spaces, no words were exchanged. It was essential that this not be turned into a demonstration against the people. It must remain focused on the justice sought by the community. Some of the staff used the designated parking lots. Others, apparently in avoidance of the news media stationed in the lots, parked four and five blocks away. Their extended walk into work that day resembled the walk the residents often made with groceries and children in tow for the past eight months. The numbers of staff members seemed exceedingly small. There appeared to be staff members who chose not to report to work that day.

Community members adhered to the request to remain silent while the staff members filed passed their homes on their way to and from work. When the media approached staff members, they were met with silence, or a simple statement of "No comment." The building administrators promised the media a prepared statement at a later time. They had no comment at the time of the broadcast. Representatives from the media promised their new contacts in the community that they would be following this story until it's conclusion.

True to their word, the print and televised media continued to follow our story. The station rebroadcast the original morning broadcast at the noon, evening, and 11:00 p.m. slots. The following two days brought additional stories. The reporters addressed the issue of inaction directly with the school board president, the district superintendent, the city road commission, and the local police department. The bicycle display remained in place; but the cause the task force had brought to the public raced forward. The justice they had fought so diligently for so long suddenly had demanded the attention of the public. They were creating their own justice. These five women had become individuals empowered to recognize social injustice and seek its downfall.

Questions

1. These women chose to demonstrate their point with a silent, static display. What is the significance of this choice for this particular group of women?

How is it reflective of this community? How will it affect the eventual outcome for the school district representatives and the community at large?

2. The involvement of the media was exceedingly effective in bringing about the change the five-woman task force had been seeking. The media promised these women they would not let the story go, and they were true to their word. The attention they were able to bring to the case was a significant factor in bringing members of the school district and the city road commission to task. Would the end results differ if these women chose to use this tactic initially?

The Community Sees Results

The bicycles were to remain in place for five days. Within two days of the onset of the display, the city road commission contacted Rae. The commissioner asked Rae if she could have the bikes removed by Thursday. The city road commission needed the space cleared to bring their equipment in. By close of the business day Thursday, signs would be in place restricting parking on the two streets in question for nonresidents. Rae notified the task force and plans were set in place to remove the display. By 4:00 p.m. Thursday afternoon, the streets were clear of bicycles, and the road signs were in place.

Friday was the first test. Restricted parking signs replaced the bicycle display. Friday saw no parking violations. The following week, two staff members were in violation of the new parking restriction. Local police, who had increased their patrols in the area, ticketed their vehicles. The weeks that followed saw no further parking violations. The five-woman task force had affectively restored order and justice to the parking situation in their community.

A Partnership Is Formed

All five women from the original task force and myself were sent invitations to a meeting with the president of the school board, the district superintendent, and president of the teacher's association. Not knowing fully what to expect, the six of us made arrangements to attend the meeting. On the day of the meeting, we were informed that the president of the teacher's association was forced to send his regrets. We met with the school board president and the district superintendent. The air of the meeting was entirely different. There were no suit coats to be seen, and refreshments had been prepared. The power differential so apparent in our last meeting was absent.

The meeting progressed with its welcoming and respectful tone. The superintendent congratulated the community members for bringing about the change that they had "all hoped for." The school board president reiterated that, while their hands had been tied, they were both impressed and grateful for the measures that the community had taken to overcome this obstacle. The task force members accepted their gratitude. They did not question the position of the district representatives. The situation had been rectified. They owned its history, and wanted to move forward. This group of women wanted to establish a working relationship with the public school district. This time the relationship would have its foundation on equal and respectful ground.

The relationship did continue. The district took measures to restore a small playground that was on the premises. No children were currently served in the building. This playground would be for the exclusive use of the community. Parking was no longer an issue for the community. The staff made use of the parking facilities provided for them. In the coming months, one staff member broke his ankle, which required crutches for six weeks. A district representative contacted Gretchen, and the community provided a parking space on the street for the employee until his ankle healed.

Where once there had been a relationship based on authority and oppression, a healthier egalitarian relationship had emerged. The five women, whose lives had been engulfed in systems of oppression, were able to bring about this emergence. The process had allowed them to find the strengths they possessed and use them effectively to advocate for themselves and their community. They gained a greater sense of empowerment, not simply from the eventual success of their efforts, but from the efforts themselves.

Questions

1. **Draw a strategic plan of the steps these women took throughout the eight-month process to bring about its eventual outcome. Try to identify tactics that were effective and those that could be readdressed. Which actions may have contributed to the healthy working relationship that these parties currently hold for one another?**

2. **These five women came to this action through systems of oppression. They continued to gain a sense of their own strengths through successes and challenges. How do you expect this journey to affect other avenues in their lives? How would you prepare them to look at these possibilities?**

3. **Take a moment to review the task force's progress. Based on the author's description, the professional literature, and the latest practice evidence, what occurred to account for the progress?**

4. **What was the theoretical approach or combination of approaches that appeared to work best?**

5. **Based on the work you have done earlier, what additional intervention(s) would you recommend? Use the literature and latest evidence to justify your recommendations.**

6. **Overall, what is your professional opinion of the work performed in this case? As always, refer to the professional literature, practice evidence, your**

experience, and the experience of student-colleagues when developing your opinion.

7. Based on this review, what additional or alternative approaches could have been used with this case? That is, if you were the practitioner, how would you have approached this case? Please explain and justify your approach.

8. What did this case demonstrate that you could use in other practice settings? List the most important things you learned by studying this case and how you could use them in your practice career.

Bibliography

Alinsky, S. A. (1972). *Rules for Radicals*. New York: Random House.
Corey, G., & Corey, M. (1997). *I never knew I had a chance* (6th ed.). Pacific Grove, CA: Sage.
Franks, V., & Burtle, V. (Eds.). (1974). *Women in therapy: New psychotherapies for a changing society*. New York: Brunner/Mazel.
Garvin, C. D., and Tropman, J. E. (1992). *Social work in contemporary society*. Englewood Cliffs, NJ: Prentice Hall.
Longres, J. F. (1990). *Human behavior and the social environment*. Itasca, IL: F. E. Peacock Publishers.
Maton, K. I. (1989). The stress-buffering role of spiritual support: Cross-sectional and prospective investigations. *Journal of Scientific Study of Religion, 28,* 310–323
Wilson, James Q., and George Kelling (1982). "The police and neighborhood safety: Broken windows." *Atlantic, 127,* 29–38.

4

Organizing Social Work in the Republic of Armenia Part I

Jerry L. Johnson

Introduction

In July 2002, an international contract agency[1] associated with USAID, the wing of the U.S. State Department responsible for humanitarian aid abroad, contacted me about a community project in the Republic of Armenia. The sponsoring organization sought a social work professional with community practice and community assessment experience, and familiarity with Armenia. Moreover, they were in a hurry. I left for Yerevan, Armenia, ten days after our initial contact, leaving little time for planning and preparation.

My assignment entailed performing a national need assessment with diverse populations in Armenia about the future of professional social work in the country. Specifically, my project's goals included the following:

1. To evaluate existing social work training capacity in Armenia and any opportunities to reinforce any current developments in this area.
2. To provide insight about where demand for trained social workers might emerge in the social sector, particularly within the government of Armenia (Ministry of Health and Social Security and their affiliated organizations working in local government).

[1] Academy for Educational Development (AED) was the sponsoring organization.

3. To recommend a technical assistance and training program to improve the professional human resource capacity of social workers that was reasonable, within the near and mid-term projections of demand in Armenia and existing financial resources.

My sponsors left decisions about how to organize the project to me, in collaboration with a local Advisory Committee consisting of various stakeholders in Armenia's healthcare and social service delivery systems. The sponsors provided four weeks total to complete this assignment, including three weeks in country and one week to complete my report and recommendations. For a project this comprehensive, three weeks in country was short. I was going to be busy on this trip!

My Relationship with Armenia

Since the fall of the Soviet Union in the early 1990s, the former satellite countries have struggled to develop new economic, political, health, and social systems to replace their former social structure. The Republic of Armenia is no exception. Since its independence in 1992, this small country in the Caucasus region has found the road from Communism to democracy simultaneously difficult and exhilarating, depending on one's social position and relationships to the changes. For those in government and business, the changes have been exhilarating; for most citizens, the years since the fall of Communism have been difficult, at best.

I first met the Armenian people in 1995 (Johnson, 1999a; 199b) as a consultant for the United Nations Development Programme (UNDP). Those were bleak days for the Armenian people, having lived through a tumultuous historical period beginning with a deadly earthquake in 1988 and ending with a blockade by neighboring countries during and after the Nagorno-Karabakh war with Azerbaijan (Johnson, 1999a). Along the way, Armenia transitioned from a relatively wealthy Soviet republic to a desperately poor independent country, surrounded by hostile neighbors, largely without food or resources, including heat and electricity. As you will discover later, my experience in Armenia during one of the most difficult periods in the country's history became an important "credential" as I returned to tackle this case.

This would be my fifth trip to this beautiful country, my first since 1998. As much as I liked the land, I thoroughly enjoyed the people, culture, and history of this small, yet significant country. Even during those bleak years in the mid-1990s I found the Armenian people to be gracious, friendly, and open hosts whose only interest was for people to understand them and their unique culture and history. I eagerly anticipated discovering what changes had occurred in my adopted second home since my last trip nearly four years earlier.

Questions

Imagine that you were hired as a consultant to perform a comprehensive community project in the Republic of Armenia. If you are like most in America, you probably know little about this country. However, before delving into the specifics of the country, this type of assignment requires advance planning. Elsewhere, the author claimed that personal considerations and issues become the most important considerations when planning and performing work in a foreign country (Johnson, 1999a, 1999b). Hence, before reading on in this case, respond to the following questions.

1. Make a list of your professional considerations as you prepare to accept this project. Include everything from theories, models, and methods to logistics, and so on.

2. Make a list of your personal considerations to prepare for this project. Discuss your experience with diverse populations at home and abroad. What personal issues and strengths do you bring to this project that relate to your ability to adjust to a different and often strange environment?

The Republic of Armenia: A Brief History

A distant republic of the former Soviet Union located in the southern Caucasus Mountains of Eastern Europe, the Republic of Armenia has maintained a distinct national and cultural identity since the seventh century BC. The Armenian people descended from ancient tribes who inhabited their traditional homeland in Eastern Anatolia during prehistoric times. There is a remarkable record of continuous human occupation of the region around Mount Ararat (today part of Turkey) since the Old Stone Age. Mount Ararat (Masis) is the legendary resting place of Noah's Ark and visible in the western skyline. As beautiful and majestic as this mountain is, it provides a constant reminder of the 1915 genocide by the Young Turks (Ottoman Empire) against the Armenian people (Miller & Miller, 1993), to all Armenians in the homeland. Armenians simultaneously love and hate Masis.

Armenia was a great power in the time of Julius Caesar (first century BC) and is the oldest Christian nation in the world, having been converted by St. Gregory in AD 301. Once dominated by Persians, Romans, Byzantine Greeks, Arabs, and Turks, the Armenians had only brief periods of independence over many thousands of years. In 1064, the Turks invaded Armenia, beginning nearly a millennium of strife between the two peoples (UNDP, 1993). The hatred between the two countries was exacerbated by the genocide in 1915 and recently by Turkey's support of Azerbaijan in the Nagorno-Karabakh conflict.

In 1920, Armenia became part of the Soviet Union for protection from further Turkish aggression and to provide the Soviets a strategic border with the Turks and the Muslim world to the south. Contemporary Armenia, which borders Turkey to the west, Georgia to the north, Azerbaijan to the east and southwest, and Iran to the south, represents only ten percent of historical Great Armenia, a fact not lost on all Armenians regardless of where they live in the world.

By end of the twentieth century, the Republic of Armenia had suffered through several tragic years. Since 1988, few countries have endured natural and human disasters as the Armenians. In December 1988, Armenia suffered a major earthquake leaving an estimated 50,000 people dead and 500,000 homeless (Verluise, 1989). Because the "earth itself shook" (Verluise, 1989, p. 103), the earthquake was even more intolerable for Armenians because of the faith they placed in their homeland as the foundation of Armenian culture and tradition. Now, even the land was unstable.

This tragedy thrust Armenia into the world spotlight, leading to an outpouring of foreign humanitarian aid. Leninakian (now called Gjumri), the second largest city in Armenia, and Spitak were completely destroyed, sending thousands of refugees fleeing for an already overcrowded Yerevan (UNDP, 1993). My colleagues in Yerevan said their city also shook that fateful day, although it experienced little damage. By 2002, much of urban areas had been rebuilt. However, the damage was still apparent outside the major cities. I addressed this issue in my field notes:

> As I heard many times, in almost all government departments, the earthquake and the earthquake zone provide the biggest challenges to the system. It either motivates the needs for services, or remains the focus of many social problems. The earthquake area has the highest unemployment, large numbers of homeless refugees, shadow employment (crime), significant health issues, high occurrences of PTSD, as well as other "disaster-related" problems.

In 1988 and early 1989, old tensions between Armenia and Azerbaijan boiled into armed conflict over the Nagorno-Karabakh region. Soviet leadership gave this mountainous region southeast of Armenia to the Azeris, although 75 percent of its population was Armenian (Malkasian, 1996). Given the Azeris' close political and religious ties to Turkey, this hotly debated issue remained dormant during the seventy years of Soviet rule. In 1989, amidst nationalistic fervor on both sides, the Azeris massacred hundreds of Armenians in the city of Sumgait, a move that ultimately led to war in 1990. Both countries have lived under a negotiated cease-fire arrangement since 1994, although there were reports of occasional bombings near the Armenian-Azerbaijan border (UNDP, 1993). As of 2002, the war had not officially ended, and Armenians remained committed to their beliefs that Nagorno-Karabakh rightly belonged to the Republic of Armenia.

In 1991, two more events almost sounded the death knell for Armenia. In September, Armenia declared independence from the Soviet Union. Literally overnight, they lost Soviet industry, protection, and economic assistance. The effects on the economy were crippling. Additionally, because of the Karabakh conflict, the Azeris and Turks imposed a blockade of Armenia. Since Armenia is a landlocked nation, this led to economic devastation.

The blockade was exacerbated by civil strife in Georgia, Abkhazia, and North Ossetia (neighboring regions), which resulted in the closure of the railroads and the gas pipeline coming from the north, leaving the Armenians reliant on outside humanitarian aid for subsistence. The country was dependent on imports of fuel resulting in a severe shortage of this commodity, which crippled the economy. There was no central heating or hot water; houses received electricity for less than two hours per day and schools closed during the winter because of the harsh weather conditions (UNDP, 1993).

The impact of the blockade was twofold. First, people were leaving Armenia. The destabilizing exodus of some 800,000 educated and resourceful Armenians, mostly young people, occurred at a time when they were needed the most for nation-building. Second, the crisis diverted Armenian energy, exuberance, and initiative to the difficult requirements of simple survival instead of nation building. By 2002, the blockade had ended, although relations with Turkey and the remainder of the Muslim world remained tense. Armenia still had difficulties importing needed goods, and the economy was slow to recover. Were it not for significant international aid and slowly forming international business investment, the Republic of Armenia's economy would collapse.

While it seems that Armenia found a semblance of political stability over the years, economically, the country continued struggling. In my 2002 field notes, I commented on the state of the Armenian economy and its people.

Here are some staggering poverty statistics for Armenia. In 1999, 230,000 families received assistance through the Armenian Family Poverty Benefit Program (FPBP). In 2002, 150,000 receive benefits. My contact said that the numbers dropped because of standards that are more rigorous and not improving economic conditions. The government needed to save money, so it changed the criteria. In fact, according to my contact, poverty had become "deeper" and more entrenched. Armenia maintains a poverty database with 350,000 families listed on it. That is, these families cannot provide for themselves in the present economy.

However, these figures become even more staggering when calculated out from number of families to number of individuals. Based on the government average of four per family, nearly 1.4 million people are considered poor and not self-sustaining—out of an estimated present population of 3.1 million people. Therefore, nearly 55% of all Armenian residents could not provide for daily needs. I learned later that the figure was revised downward to 51%.

Even public support provided little relief. For example, an FPBP worker, based on the family's financial condition, scores each family on a continuum from zero to 72. The higher the score, the poorer is the family. Since the program's inception in 1999, scores of 36 and above qualified families for a monthly benefit of 4000 dram (approx. $7.70 USD) plus 1700 dram (approx $3 USD) per child under 18 years old. Therefore, a family of four (average size) receives $14 per month ($3.50 per person per month). Marina today estimated that it costs approximately $50 per person per month for basic living needs in present-day Armenia.

Families that score above 36 (36.1 and higher) can qualify for what is called a "State Grant." This is a one-time grant of 4000 dram to help in a time of crisis, or as a precursor to a family's approval for FPBP. As an aside, KM and DT stated that 90% of kids in Armenia's five state-run orphanages have parents and family. They are placed because parents cannot financially support their children. Additionally, current health care funding allocates approximately $7 to $8 USD per person, per year for health care funding.

The quadruple shock of earthquake, loss of the all-controlling Soviet state, the death and destruction of war, and the isolation and deprivation caused by the blockade and slow economic progress had turned Armenia in on itself and numbed the hopes of a people yearning for a successful, independent future.

Moreover, Armenia's geographic location suggests several geopolitical issues at present. Each of these issues is part of an overall multi-systemic approach to community practice in this country. Geographically, Armenia is located near Iraq and Iran, sits as the only Christian nation among many Muslim neighbors, and has a long history of hostile relations with Turkey, a significant U.S. ally. Additionally, Armenia is located southwest of Chechnya, the hotly contested region in southern Russia. In the past, Armenia enjoyed the sole support of the United States in its battles with Azerbaijan. However, with the discovery of mass stores of oil in the Caspian Sea off the Azeri coast, U.S. diplomats began dialogue with Azerbaijan, to the dismay of the Armenian people.

Questions

Before proceeding with this case, your task is to "discover" Armenia for yourself. Please respond to the following questions, either alone or in small groups.

1. Locate the Republic of Armenia on a map. By examining its geographic location and its neighbors, what initial ideas do you have about the country and the geopolitical issues involved for the Armenians?

2. Examine the professional literature to locate information about Armenia and its history, people, culture, and economic issues. Develop a five-page synopsis of the country, focusing on its relevant history, culture (including religion), economics, and problems. Moreover, from your reading, identify several of the country's strengths that may be useful in completing this task.

3. Specifically, research the Armenian genocide of 1915 and the Nagorno-Karabakh war. Consider how these events might link in contemporary times in the minds of the Armenian people to affect the country's current situation.

Arrival

I had only one rule for my sponsoring organization: I refused to fly Armenian Airlines unless it was the only airline flying to the country. In the past, Armenian Airlines was the only way into the country by air. Elsewhere (Johnson, 1999a), I describe my experiences with this airline and its one airplane, the notorious Tupalev 154. This airplane was a staple of Aeroflot, the airline of the former Soviet Union.

These planes were "known" for crashing, and Armenian Airlines did not have the budget to keep it maintained properly. I had flown on this airplane eight times and figured that perhaps my luck was running out. Graciously, my sponsors booked me on a reputable international carrier. Whew! I later learned that Armenian Airlines was grounded because of poor maintenance and the generally poor condition of its airplane. Western airport authorities refused to allow the airplane to land at their facilities.

Early in the morning of the first day, my local contact rang my hotel to arrange an initial meeting that day. During our meeting, Marina, my contact, provided operational details and discussed the advisory panel that I would meet early the next morning. After this meeting, I began my preparations for this large and potentially unwieldy project before falling asleep early. I had a meeting scheduled with the Advisory Committee early the next morning. This meeting marked my first and only opportunity to make a favorable first impression and begin establishing my credibility with the local committee. I would need their support if I were to accomplish my goals over the next three weeks.

Monday, July 22: The Advisory Committee

When I perform community work, my main instrument is usually personal and/or group interviews, participant observation, and a detailed and lengthy field journal (notes). I record notes throughout the day, describing various meetings, people, locations, environments, and so on. Every night, I take as long as I need to make a detailed recording of the day's activities, including personal issues and questions. Later, as I answer questions, learn new information, change my perspectives, and/or discover ideas for later use, I update the journal. That is, I ask myself questions and make notes to myself about people, relationships, and my impressions and feelings about the day's work. When I finish projects, my field notes provide a running and interactive commentary about the experience, making it easier to prepare reports, presentations, and even chapters for casebooks.

In the following passage, I describe the first meeting of the Advisory Committee. I took these notes directly from my field notes, but have changed the names and initials to preserve confidentiality. Since these are my notes, they are my personal reconstruction of what occurred and not a representation of the "Truth." That is, my notes represent my recollection of the events, filtered through my reality, values, and beliefs about people, groups, and circumstances. In addition, since I took the following passage directly from my notes, I apologize in advance for the format and potential improper sentence construction. I left the notes "as is" to demonstrate their use and content in real form.

Field Notes: Monday, July 22, 2002

> Before I begin, I need to answer some questions for myself. What is my relationship with this committee? What is their expectation about their responsibility or authority over the project and my actions?

First, I learned before the meeting that it is an advisory committee. I am responsible to (my sponsor) and not the committee. It is supposed to help with data collection, access to key people and information, and offer critical reactions and reflections regarding outcomes. What is not clear is the relationship between the committee and my final report. Do they have the power to determine how it should read, or what it should say . . . both, or neither? This will be important to understand as I move through the process.

My only formal contact with the committee occurred in this meeting. I meet again with the committee on Wednesday, 8/7 (day before I leave), to present my draft report and executive summary for review and feedback. That will be an interesting meeting, indeed.

In attendance: SR, Marina, FM (USAID), KB (PDOO), Sue (YSU), GR (Advisor to Minister-MOSS), GG (Deputy Head of Social Services Dept—MOSS), and MH (PDOO Training & Pilot Project Consultant). Missing was representatives of Ministry of Health (MOH) and HL, the Head of Social Work Program at the local university.

First, some historical background offered by SR, head of my sponsoring organization. I was most interested in the relationship between FM, the working group, and my project. In his opening remarks, FM spent 15 minutes telling me (with others watching) what the project was about, changing the written terms I agreed to ever so subtly. According to SR, FM is an outside consultant to USAID and the director of the larger health care reform project managed by PDOO. He contracts the operation of this project to PDOO, the organization responsible for implementing the massive changes in Armenia's health care system as a contract agency to USAID. That made FM the final authority on my project. I need to understand FM's agenda.

My project originated through ideas forwarded by KB from PDOO. As a social worker, KB was interested in making social work an integral part of the social services in Armenia. According to SR, he was someone with "big ideas" (idealistic) and sometimes did not come off as practical, despite not becoming angry if things do not immediately go his way.

So, KB (working with HL from the university) approached USAID and my sponsoring organization to provide social work training to all Ministry of Social Services (MOSS) workers at the 55 local offices all over Armenia through a "social work summer school" (not a bad idea, actually). Their recommendation was based on a study conducted by a British consultant one year earlier. According to SR, my sponsor was set to provide this training and financial support to HL for distance education training. As of June (one month prior), FM was "on board" with this project. Then, in the interim between the unofficial go-ahead for this project and now, FM apparently changed his mind, deciding that he could not fund the training project until there was an evaluation completed (that's I). As such, HL comes to this project feeling "burned" by this turn of events, as one might expect.

Be aware of this dynamic and join with HL through our joint interest in SW. If she is cool and hostile, work through it as part of the context of the assessment. Also, remain aware that KB's interest, according to SR, is in moving full speed ahead on a country-wide SW training course throughout the MOSS and the Ministry of Health (MOH). This explains the focus on government agencies. I am being paid by funds originally going to their project. They have every right to feel burned and be resistant at first. I must overcome this quickly.

Now, turning to the meeting, my goals for this meeting were to meet a few people, get an initial read on FM, and schedule a few meetings to begin the process. I purposely said little in the meeting, trying to position myself as a learner and listener.

FM, in his opening remarks, stated that the project was "simple" to him. He said that I should forget the issue of "need" as there was "always need." The issue here was "demand" for social work. Is there a demand for SW services and is it possible and practical to develop a way to train only more "outreach" or caseworkers"? That is, forget social work training per se, and (if there is a practical demand) focus on creating a sustainable way to provide simple and basic training to give workers fundamental outreach worker skills (i.e., certificate programs leading to paraprofessional status), all of whom could be "supervised" by qualified social workers. He didn't say where these qualified social workers to do the training and supervision would come from. He did say that he doubts the existence of a SW culture, although he left that statement vague. I need to follow up on this statement during our private meeting tomorrow (7/23/02). He also said that he was interested in issues related to licensing and accreditation.

Sue from YSU was representing HL, head of the social work department at the state university. She did not have much to say other than the "distance education" program was the hot commodity. She mentioned that there were six (6) lessons completed (in Armenian) that were not available in English. I asked for copies of these lessons, and she stated that she would discuss this with HL. Sue also stated that there were 140 trained social workers working in Armenia. She did not respond to my inquiry about whether these were the number of graduates, or working social workers.

KB from PDOO discussed his integral role in helping social work become accepted in his country as a central part of the social insurance and government programs. He seemed to have the same vision for Armenia. While SW is not a known entity and probably will not be accepted at first (by clients, systems, or both?) a process can occur to make that happen.

He had a representative from PDOO's "training the trainer" initiative in the meeting (MH) and he seemed to be wondering, without really saying it in the meeting, if SW training could be accomplished and carried out in local MOSS centers by the trainers, trained through PDOO to provide local training. This has some possibilities, yet—can non-social workers learn the skills well enough to provide competent training after a six-week, six-month, or even a one-year training certificate program? He also spoke about the distance education program that began through a cooperative with Open University of Oxford and the Irish Association of Social Workers. Perhaps I need to see these folks too.

He seems like a competent fellow with great ideas. In fact, if SR is correct, his desire to make sweeping change fits with my notion of how change should occur, while FM seems to be saying, "Don't shake things up too much." Differences in style, personality, ethnicity/social traditions, or role in the project (KB is the implementer while FM is the representative of the institutional system that is invariably conservative it its approach), or perhaps sweeping change makes FM feel as if he is losing control of his project. Probably the answer lies in a mix of all of this.

I am encouraged about the state of social work education and training at this point. Lessons and materials already developed in Armenian, and not in English. It is usually the opposite. Perhaps HL and her program are further along on adapting SW principles to Armenian culture and its political, economic, and social realities than I would have believed before arriving.

As the end of the meeting approached, GG and GR from MOSS each spoke at length about social work and their backgrounds. GG stated that this was a good idea, but there was no local funding for all of this. GR essentially told his resume in Armenian government (back 40 years to Communist period) and said nothing much more, mainly because time was running out and people began to interrupt.

It was an interesting dynamic, one that I must observe more fully, and—if true—avoid participating in at all costs. The dynamic was this: when FM, KB, or SR (and, I guess that will mean me) spoke, all were quiet and listening. When the Armenians began speaking, the English speakers began speaking to each other while the Armenians were speaking. Almost as if what the Armenians had to say was not important. Not only was this disrespectful, but ethnocentric. It wouldn't surprise me if this were a common occurrence. Therefore, observe and work to counteract this occurrence in meetings with the Armenians.

Today's meeting ended with the scheduling of meetings with these people over the next two days.

Comments about Field Notes

In the above passage, I covered the basic elements that I recorded in my field notes. While there are important issues that all community workers ought to record, each practitioner develops his or her own style and format for ease of use and maximum efficiency. Typically, I record important facts and data stated in meetings. However, perhaps you noticed that I focused less on what members actually said than I did on the dynamics involved in the group process.

In addition to community assessment and interventions skills, I believe that community or international practitioners must be adept at understanding group dynamics in cultural context and at working with groups. In community settings, most everything practitioners do occurs with groups, from assessment to intervention and follow-up. Therefore, I encourage students interested in community practice to hone their group practice skills, focusing on understanding group dynamics and knowing how to create a productive context in groups as a leader.

I generally include different levels of information in my field notes, each denoted by its own format. That is, I include personal observations and perceptions (indented text) and responses to observations and perceptions (*underlined text*). When I include an idea for later use or possible intervention, I use bold text to denote these items. This is my formatting formula, making my field notes easier for me to use effectively during my projects.

I adopted these techniques for community practice from my work as an ethnographer (Johnson, 1999a; Wolcott, 1995; Agar, 1980). That is, I use skills from research, mainly participant observation (DeWalt, DeWalt, & Wayland, 1998), as the basis for all community practice, whether I practice in a local neighborhood, among a group of workers fighting for their rights, or in a foreign country.

Research as Practice; Practice as Research

While my sponsors and I believed that this was primarily a research project, I approached it the same as any other community practice or community change project. I believe that all research is practice, and all practice is research. That is, I reject the dichotomy in many professional schools and settings between research and practice; both must integrate to form a multi-systemic whole. This is true in the field and in my classrooms. Hence, I teach research classes as if they are social work practice courses and teach research and research methods as integral parts of traditional practice classes.

I find that most qualitative methods, especially ethnography, parallels the process used in practice with individuals, couples, families, groups, and communities. Therefore, research classes allow students the opportunity to improve their case planning, interviewing, observation, data collection, data analysis, summarization, and report writing skills for practice, as well as learn important research and evaluation skills. Moreover, most students have stopped "hating" research.

Community Practice Approaches

In the early days of the profession, social work concerned itself primarily with reform movements, organizing, social policy advocacy, and the rights of disenfranchised groups. In short, as a profession, social work's original roots were in community practice, sometimes called "macro practice" (Shulman, 1999, p. 764). However, over the course of the twentieth century, social work moved away from its roots to an individualistic, clinical focus (Zastrow, 2003).

Fellin (1995) defined three types of communities: those based on geographical location, non-place communities of identification (race, gender, sexual orientation, etc.), and personal communities comprising the multiple communities of each individual and/or group. In a community practice setting, practitioners must consider each of these elements and their interactions before planning intervention (Johnson, 2004). See my earlier work for an ethnographic account of my experience in Armenia and an in-depth view of Armenian culture in the context of the mid to late 1990s (Johnson, 1999a).

Rothman and Tropman (1995) categorized community practice into three "ideal" approaches: locality development, social planning, and social action. While these are ideal types, actual community practice integrates aspects of each into practice.

The locality-development, also known as community development, suggests that community change best happens through broad-based participation of a cross section of people in the community, including the disadvantaged and members of the power structure (Zastrow, 2003; Rothman & Tropman, 1995). It focuses on dialogue and communication between factions in a community to reach consensus on which problems to focus on and which strategies to use to resolve these problems.

Social planning assumes that community change requires highly trained and skilled planners who can guide complex change processes. The expert is highly regarded and organizes data, analyzes data, serves as program planners, implementers, and facilitators. Since the expert usually works for the prevailing power structure, he or she tends to serve the interest of that structure, usually by avoiding radical change or controversial recommendations. Generally, regular members of the target community are not part of a social planning process. At best, they participate peripherally.

Social action assumes that the disadvantaged or oppressed members of a community must be organized to pressure the power structure to increase resources or for social justice (Zastrow, 2003). Social action approaches seek basic changes in the power structure and/or in basic policies of institutions. Social action assumes an adversarial relationship between the people and power structure.

Questions

The author has presented several ideas about approaching a project such as the Armenian need assessment. Before moving on in this case, take a few minutes to respond to the following questions and complete the following exercises.

1. Many people believe that researchers, even participant observers, must approach the research act in an objective and dispassionate manner. That is, researchers should not become active change agents as part of the research process. Others believe differently; researchers should push for change, especially pertaining to social and economic justice. Examine the literature on epistemology and the purpose and function of research, looking for arguments from both sides of this dilemma. Compare and contrast the various positions. What does the Code of Professional Ethics (NASW, 2000) say about this issue, if anything at all?

2. Given the nature of this project and the statements of the author above, what position is the author taking on this argument? Please explain.

3. Examine literature on ethnography as a method of social research. Compare the methods and issues in ethnography to the literature about the

methods and issues for practice. In your opinion, are they comparable? In other words, develop an informed critique of the author's statement that "research is practice and practice is research."

4. Examine the literature on community practice further, developing a more in-depth understanding than what the author provided above. Based on your readings, under what category of community practice does this project fall? If needed, integrate the ideal types presented above to address the function and intention of the author in this case.

Developing a Plan of Action

Given that I only had three weeks to complete this assignment, I needed to formulate a plan of action overnight. During the next three weeks, I had to gather enough data from enough people in different social and professional locations to provide credibility to the findings, write a report, and present it to the Advisory Committee and the head of the U.S. Mission to Armenia.

In consultation with the Advisory Committee and sponsors, I adapted a two-pronged approach to data collection. First, I would attempt to interview as many key informants as possible. I define key informants as those people or groups that, based on their profession or experience, could speak most directly to the subject at hand. Therefore, I sought the names of heads of departments, hospitals, social service programs, and important NGOs around Armenia. My contact in the sponsor's office was responsible for arranging the meetings and developing a list of important people to interview.

Secondly, I employed a snowball sampling procedure. That is, I asked each person or group I interviewed to identify others that may be important people to interview. Here, I wanted to find lay professionals and/or clients to interview. I did not want to be relegated to speaking only to professional people. I wanted to provide policymakers and funding sources with feedback from the targets of the services. This strategy worked, as I was able to find several NGOs and clients willing to meet and discuss the issues outside the context of my sponsor's agenda.

I intended to interview everyone face-to-face, in his or her offices and/or homes as appropriate. I wanted to spend the majority of my time traveling and interviewing, trying to meet as many different people as possible in three weeks. Each night, I would write my recollections of the day's meetings in my field notes and formulate new questions, ideas, or new people that I needed to meet the next day or week.

Language Issues

While I had worked in Armenia several times before, I am not Armenian, nor do I speak the Armenian language. I learned enough language to "get around" on my own, but not nearly enough to converse. Hence, I required a skilled interpreter to participate in every meeting, someone who could spend an inordinate amount of time with me over the next three weeks. This person needed to have a basic under-standing of social services to communicate meaning and ideas correctly.

Moreover, I needed to trust my interpreter. Elsewhere (Johnson, 1999a), I write at length about language and problems with translation in professional set-tings. On previous trips to Armenia, I used the same interpreter for each project. Over the years, we developed an excellent working relationship that blossomed into a personal friendship. However, on this trip my regular interpreter was unavailable. She worked full time and could not break away to take short-term employment with my sponsor. I had to find a new interpreter and hope to develop a relationship that allowed me to trust that my statements were translated accurately and vice versa. On my first trip, my work hit a roadblock with an important person in the medical sys-tem when I later learned that the interpreter purposely mistranslated my statements to the doctor, and the doctor's statements to me, leading to a major misunderstand-ing (Johnson, 1999a). I discovered from another person that this interpreter had a personal and professional "stake" in the meeting, so she told each of us what she wanted to say, not what actually was said in the meeting. I did not want this to hap-pen again.

After cycling through two different interpreters (one who had too many opin-ions and one that did not tell me what others were saying), I luckily found a terrif-ic interpreter that I worked closely with for the majority of my time there. She did not understand social services but was an honest interpreter and a "quick study." Our relationship developed to the point where I could ask her about people's intentions, meaning, and hidden agendas. In short, she did more than interpret language. She began interpreting body language and hidden meanings that only someone from the culture and fluent in the language would understand. She became an invaluable assistant in this project.

Activist Approach

I approached this project from an activist standpoint. That is, depending on the find-ings, I wanted to have an effect by creating or stimulating change. I did not want my report to end up in a pile of expensive consultant reports that collect dust in some bureaucrat's office. Hence, I needed to collect enough information and establish enough credibility so that people in decision-making capacities actually read and considered the findings. If I discovered a need and demand for social work, I want-ed to create the context where the appropriate bureaucracies would take action. I was hopeful that this project would garner serious consideration.

Project Information

The social work need assessment project grew out of a larger reform effort in Armenia. USAID and the World Bank funded a major, five-year overhaul of the healthcare and social service systems in Armenia. These organizations wanted to reform the former Soviet system, eliminate bureaucratic levels, and ensure more immediate and useful service to the Armenian population while saving money through efficiency. PDOO administered the overall healthcare reform project. PDOO was an international contract agency experienced in healthcare reform.

Under contract with USAID, PDOO administered every aspect of the reform. As stated in my field notes earlier, KB was the PDOO employee responsible for social service reform. KB wanted a significant role for the social work profession in government social services, especially in the Armenian "welfare" system. Presently, MOSS workers in the 55 Marz (Armenian for county or state) handled all aspects of the FPBP, yet they had no background or training in human services. KB believed that the future of the social service system hinged largely on providing a well-trained workforce, based on fundamental social work education, training, and professional values.

Below are several excerpts from my field notes that describe the various roles, responsibilities, and experiences of those serving in "social work" positions in the Ministry of Social Services (MOSS) in Armenia at the time of the project.

Meetings at MOSS (GG)

GG is the deputy head of the social services department. She explained the Family Poverty Benefit Program (FPBP) at length. The FPBP is administered through the 55 local MOSS offices in the various regions (Marz) of Armenia. According to GG, here is how the program works:

1. Families in need apply for benefits at the local FPBP office, on a two-page application.
2. The FPBP inspector (social worker) investigates the family's application, which includes a home visit. According to GG, the worker has up to 25 days to investigate and make a recommendation to approve or deny benefits. There is one worker per district, with each having primary responsibility of somewhere between 500 and 1000 families receiving the benefits. According to GG, these workers (Poverty Family Benefit inspectors) also serve in a general "case management" capacity for the families. GG stated that they are "trained professionals" that earn approximately $35 per month, and mostly serve as the "welfare police," trying to find ways to deny benefits and save on the federal budget.
3. GG claimed that the inspectors were "highly trained" professionals who did not need outside help or training.

GR: Advisor to the Minister of MOSS and Coordinator of Training in MOSS

GR had a lot to say about training and the training needs of the MOSS staff. He said—unlike GG—that the training level of staff is poor and that everyone needs extensive training in MOSS.

He also said that if there are 140 trained social workers (figure given by Sue from YSU in Advisory Committee meeting) that perhaps as few as two or three actually work for MOSS. He sees this as a failure of MOSS personnel policy and recruitment strategies.

> I'm sure that it has little to do with this in fact. My guess is that these people, if they are working at all in social work, are working for NGOs or other international organizations (such as AED, UNDP, etc.) that pay better and allow work that is more along the line of social work, beyond case management. Others are most likely (my guess, this would be most) in other professions, from teachers to other type of work with NGOs and international organizations. Why go to work for government bureaucracy for $35 per month?

Meeting with KB @ PDOO: 7/24/02

KB's focus is particularly on MOSS and the need for workers in that agency. He is the mover on the integrated social service site (ISS) in Vanadzor, although the site is not open yet.

The ISS is a pilot program designed to bring all MOSS services under one roof, hoping to make service delivery easier and friendlier. KB and the local organizing group have met about this project for over one year, and it is yet to open. He is also working to get NGO representation on the grounds of the service sites to facilitate public/private cooperation in MOSS service delivery. Pertaining to the information gathered yesterday at MOSS, he stated:

1. Inspectors do not have 700 to 1000 clients to see regularly. They spend 3 months qualifying recipients each year, and then do nothing for the rest of the year. Therefore, it would be possible for them to serve in a case manager or triage capacity with their clients in need.
2. He claims that most of the inspectors in the districts are untrained and open to new training. He said they are dedicated people who would like to find ways to help. This is encouraging.

KB painted a better picture about MOSS inspectors than the other interviewees did. He viewed them as eager for training, interested in helping, and not overworked. Everyone else, including the workers, viewed themselves differently. GG was the only respondent I met during my time in the country that believed the workers were well trained. Even the workers knew that they were untrained. Of course, GG had a personal stake in that argument, as the Deputy Director of MOSS. Alternatively, GR (director of MOSS training) claimed that everyone in MOSS was untrained. Of course, as the director of training, GR's personal stake at that time was to find training money. By claiming that his workers needed training, he could justify his job in the future by finding funds for training.

7/24: Children and Family Department Meeting

I met with the Children, Family, and Women Department Head (GL), plus her immediate staff (TA and PG). This government department is comprised of two sections: issues pertaining to women, and issues pertaining to families and children.

1. Women: There are no specific services for women in either the public or private sector. The NGOs, they claim, are doing more studies than services. Therefore, this department focuses on drafting and passing legislation that targets abuses of women and to make Armenia more favorable for women. They said that a "National Program for Women's Issues" would be compiled and released soon. I think this is some kind of study or legislative agenda, but I'm not sure—and I'm not sure that these women knew either.
2. Children: The focus of this department is the five state-run orphanages. They have large staffs (I was told as many as 70 staff for 100 kids per orphanage) but none are trained in human services or social work. The staff serves as babysitters and the children do not receive professional services.

The women reported that adoption services have begun slowly in Armenia. That is, in some of the outlying Marz areas, a few children have been adopted within Armenia. One task of this department is to develop and maintain a centralized registration database for adoption. The women did not believe there were any foreign adoption programs operating in Armenia. They also reported that there is a need to examine the areas of trafficking of children and child labor, as well as street children.

3. Our longest discussion regarded the need for foster care programs in Armenia. They stated that a French group (NGO, foundation?) had begun working with the department to develop a foster care system and place children in foster families. However, the project stopped because there is no legislation to make foster care available and/or legal in Armenia.

GL also stated that there is movement to pass Family and Marriage legislation later this year. After that, as I understood it, work would begin on foster care legislation. I asked if the foster care legislation was contained in the Family and Marriage legislation, and they said that it was not included.

However, they stated clearly that when this occurs, there would be significant need for well-trained specialists in the foster care arena. That is, with this portion of the child welfare system developing (adoption and foster care), there is an inevitable demand for social work specialists in the Republic of Armenia.

> The whole area of child protection and child welfare is new here. However, it is beginning to come on, especially in recent years as people began leaving Armenia for Russia and the West; many were unwilling to take their children.
>
> I was told about a case recently where a man dropped his newborn daughter off at one of the MOSS offices because, "I don't have money to feed another child, espe-

cially another female child." (He had two older daughters). As KB stated, the only option for this family was an orphanage. The system had no services to offer, nothing to help the family stay together, or to provide the child a foster family. She was sent to an orphanage where she can expect to remain until she is 18 years old.

JB: Chief of the Department for Disabled Citizens in Armenia (Also, Programs for Elderly)

For the disabled, JB administers a three-tiered department that includes:

1. Prevention and education about disabilities. I think this had to do with legislation, and the new project underway all over Yerevan to rebuild curbs and sidewalks to make them more accessible for the disabled. This is a major project occurring at present.
2. Determining official categories of disability via teams of medical specialists all over Armenia. This system is politically and financially driven. First, JB states that disabled children less than 16 years old are not categorized. They receive financial benefits if their family qualifies for the FPBP. This makes one more task for the FPBP inspectors, this time in conjunction with MOH.

JB also said that Armenia had more than 1200 children in Yerevan alone that are isolated in apartments and cannot leave their home. She said that she has 60 staff persons who visit these clients in-home. As it turns out, they are the same FPBP inspectors.

Director of MOSS Monitoring Department

This department provides monitoring, oversight (evaluation) of the MOSS programs, as well as looks for gaps and contradictions in MOSS policy and procedure. They assess efficiencies, aspects of social situation, and the legal frameworks.

1. As I have heard many times, in almost all departments, the earthquake and the earthquake zone provide the biggest challenges to the system. It either motivates the needs for services, or remains the focus of many social problems. For example, in that area is high unemployment, a large number of refugees, shadow employment, health issues, PTSD, and other disaster-related problems.
2. He stated the need for new unemployment laws for the following reasons: Presently there are over 130,000 registered unemployed, while only 6000 people receive benefits. He claims this is because of policy and law. While I am sure that FM and others would say it is mainly because of reduced budgets. That is, the Armenian government can only pay the number of people for which they have funds.
3. In terms of training needs, he states that people have been cut off from new developments and need retraining in a multidisciplinary manner. He says that

the MOSS workforce is ill prepared to handle the challenges and issues of social problems, and that this is, perhaps, the most important area for future development, except for the creation of new jobs and industry.

Social Work Outside of MOSS

My project took me into other areas as well. In addition to MOSS, I also examined social work in the Ministry of Health (MOH), nongovernmental organizations (NGOs), and state-operated mental health, psychiatric, elderly, and youth programs across Armenia. Their feedback on social work as a profession and training needs echoed what was stated above.

Ministry of Health—Meeting with Dr. SK and Dr. PV, the Head of MOH Medical Services

We discussed a new four-year pilot project called "Psychiatric Consulting Service" with MSF Corporation that targets ways to remove and place long-term chronic psychiatric patients at Sevan Psychiatric Hospital back into the community. This project proposes—to the "socially ill" or those with mental disorders—to provide social support for client reentry into their homes and communities. I am told that Sevan Psychiatric Hospital is the place where the most chronic patients are sent, the ones that will never leave the institution—remains from old policies of Soviet times and, unfortunately, of past eras in the United States.

SK and PV gave the following information:

1. Historically (Soviet times) the policy was to hide the sick and disabled by placing people into two categories: the curable (rehab) and incurable (hidden).
2. This attitude has been changing since independence, begun mainly in Children's Services, primarily after the earthquake.
3. From the change in attitude came issues such as a "team approach" and the notion of multidisciplinary teams comprised of doctors, psychologists, lawyers, parents, and so on.
4. PV stated that they do not employ social workers in the medical system presently, mainly because of funding. PV stated that these workers would be especially useful in psychiatric hospitals, the Republican Narcology Center (drug treatment), and as part of a soon to be emerging area of hospice services. His suggestion that social workers be used as outreach workers, aftercare workers, and in-home workers to help ease the transition of patients from hospitals to the community were especially helpful and interesting.

Dr. SK, head of medical services for reproductive health in Armenia, was most open to the use of "specially trained" social workers in certain areas of her work. She stated that she is trying to implement a new method in national pregnancy and prenatal care. The research on this method, according to SK, clearly demonstrates that those who receive psychosocial support during pregnancy have fewer problems, improved delivery, and that mother and baby's adjustment is improved. She thought that this is an excellent role for social workers with "very specialized training" in this type of service delivery.

Department of Social Work at Yerevan State University

A major part of this project involved the department of social work at Yerevan State University. Its director, HL, was a talented and influential woman, who opened the social work department some years earlier. She had excellent political connections and a drive to succeed in helping social work become a major professional force in the social service system in her country. However, I entered my first meeting with her wary. My trip and project was funded to check and verify her department's capabilities and to determine whether her idea for training was possible and needed. I return to my field notes to describe our first meeting.

Meeting with HL, the Director of the Social Work Program at YSU

HL is the founder of the social work profession in Armenia, beginning with a hotline for survivors immediately following the earthquake in 1989. This was the first social work intervention in Armenian history. During this time, HL said that many social workers came to Armenia from the Diaspora, all meaning to help with the relief effort. At that time, an Armenian-American social worker from the University of Connecticut named Gabret came and began working with children in the earthquake zone.

His influence led to contact with the Dean of the School of Social Work at University of Connecticut. Through collaboration with UConn in 1993 and 1994, HL developed a six-month social work training program housed in the Sociology Department at YSU. As an aside, during my 1995 visit HL had to cancel our only meeting.

In 1995, HL established the first Social Work specialization at YSU to train SW specialists. After a multi-year struggle, she finally convinced the Ministry of Education to place social work on the "list" of approved degree programs, thereby receiving status as a bachelor's degree program in Armenia (must be about 1999). Since that time, with the help of a grant from the UK (Open University), they also began a master's degree program. To date, 140 students have graduated from the bachelor's program while the first four students graduated this past spring (2002) from the master's degree program.

A second, four-year grant helped her establish a "distance education" program network, with sites in five regions in Armenia (YSU, Lori, earthquake zone, and in two other, unnamed areas). I visit the site in Lori Marz (Vanadzor) on Tuesday. Here, with the help of the Open University, HL developed a social work training course for budding social workers, as well as a social work training course for teachers. HL also said that two-month training courses are available, tailored to the specific needs of whatever organization requests the training.

HL has two long term goals for social work:

1. Developing an "Armenian" style social work profession, along with related theory and practice methods. To this end, she has tried to have multidisciplinary meetings that have not gone well, in her estimation. Too many turf issues to date, inside and outside Armenia. She stated that the international "experts" had trouble with the idea of shaping social work to fit the Armenian tradition and culture. So much for cultural competence, huh?

2. Since she believes that Armenian social work is advanced compared to other Caucasus countries, HL wants to begin a Regional social work training and practice center that serves Armenia, Georgia, and Azerbaijan. She and a colleague recently went to a social work conference in Georgia and were impressed with their efforts. The Azeri initiative will probably generate controversy, but she believes it will help with reconciliation between the countries following the war.

HL claims that the government employs "700" people they call social workers, although not one of them is really a social worker. That is, the government calls them this, but has no idea what a social worker does. These people, therefore, are not trained. She performed focus groups with government "social workers" and found that none of them had training and most were not even trained in other professions that required interpersonal skills.

HL also said that the Nephrology Clinic has employed social workers, one in the schools in Yerevan, and some work with the Armenian Fund for Health with street children. She claims that she has had discussions with the Ministry of Justice in hopes of placing students in the prisons either for practicum and/or as employees.

Classroom Meeting with 30 Current Distance Education Students and Private Meetings with 1 Master's Degree Graduate, 1 Distance Education Graduate, and HL

I spoke with a class of distance education students. There were approximately 30 students in the class, all currently employed as teachers in local schools. The creative notion here is that if teachers learn about social work skills, they will be able to do a better job in the classroom dealing with difficult and slower learning students.

After a short discussion of school social work in the United States, I took questions and asked them about their program. The problem with this setting was that HL was present during this questioning. In fact, one older woman that knows her stood to make a speech. To her credit, HL asked her to stop. Generally, students reported learning much about social work theory. In fact, I asked questions during my talk, including what the purposes of group work with children is, and many students knew exactly what the answer was.

I was impressed with their enthusiasm and interest, especially given that HL claims these students were disinterested in the courses and without energy, only one week earlier. The issues here like the issue throughout the review of social work education and training is what practice experience and applied knowledge is available, and how practical is it for this to happen. Without practical skill building, there can be no application of social work skills. In addition, why the lectures on history and methods, and not a focus on engagement skills and assessment skills being the primary focus of the training?

Meeting with Master's Degree Graduate, Distance Education Graduate, and a Worker at a Local Orphanage

The woman who graduated from YSU stated that her education was comprehensive, and it prepared her to work afterward. She is currently employed by the distance education site in Vanadzor. I asked particularly about field practice. She stated that she had three incidents of field education over the final three years of study. HL (over lunch) stated that the first field placement is an observation of various agencies, the second is a more intensive observation, and the third places students into direct field practice for four months, three days per week.

This graduate said that in her four-month practicum working in women's reproductive health, she learned how to write case histories, and perform general casework and play therapy. She also said that she learned basic counseling skills. She did not speak about the form or method of practice supervision, which appears to be an issue.

The master's degree consists of seven courses and a thesis (diploma) on a particular area of interest to the student. This student is doing her work in women's reproductive health.

The distance education graduate claimed that her education was excellent and that she has become the director of a local NGO because of her experience. The distance education program consists of six modules, including social work history, basic skills of social work (2), social work and human rights, and something else. I will learn this later when and if HL arranges for me to receive copies of her curriculum.

Meeting with FD and Vosket at MSF

This was an informative and interesting meeting, perhaps the most relevant and informative meeting I have had so far, pertaining directly to social work practice, training, and education. MSF provides in-home and street social work services for street children and their families in Yerevan. While serving in the role of social worker here, FD is, in fact, an anthropologist. However, my opinion is that he is a skilled and knowledgeable social worker. His training in anthropology is apparent, and we share many of the same perspectives.

Briefly, this program does the following:

1. Developed two categories of street children:
   a. Children in the street: These are children who have families and homes, but spend their time in the street begging or selling, and so on, often put up to this by parents. FD claimed that these kids earn as much as 50,000 dram per year. This far exceeds state benefits. Hence, the financial incentive for families to keep children in streets is significant.
   b. Children from the street: These would be children who actually live in the streets, have no families; the traditional "street children" I see so much of in Albania and other places. FD claims that there are very few, if any, children from the streets in Armenia.

The focus of this program, therefore, is children in the streets. The staff works in the streets with the children and families, trying to provide a full range of social work services for these children and families.

2. Base all their work on a multidisciplinary team approach, consisting of social workers, doctors, psychologists, lawyers, and so on.
3. FD claims that social workers in this country come to him untrained. He also said that good, solid, and relevant training is difficult to locate. He stated the following issues related specifically to social work training in Armenia:
   a. Need to focus on concrete case management skills, not how to perform individual therapy based in psychoanalytic theory.
   b. Focus on listening skills, leading to understanding others while coming to understand self. In other words, help social workers learn the importance of doing self-work regarding stereotypes, moral judgments, and so on. Learn to be open about negative feelings about clients and how to handle these in a professional manner.
   c. Casework skills, including assessments, social histories, treatment plans, and case notes. He says that social workers coming from school do not understand case recording as a mechanism for remaining organized, systematic, and consistent in approach across a team context with cases.
   d. Also need to learn relevant psychological and social psychological issues, but must also learn the difference between casework on a team, and being a psychologist.
   e. Understand people's rights, laws, and policies, as well as the mechanisms and procedures for benefits, and so on, as most people (laypeople and professionals) do not know these things.

I also met an Armenian "social worker" on this team. He has been part of the team for two years and has gained valuable experience. Vosket is FD's assistance coordinator, and had excellent comments about social work and training needs/skills required for future social workers. All of Vosket's social work training has come on the job. He is a former history teacher with no formal social work training. Yet, he is one of the most experienced social workers I have met in Armenia.

Vosket provided the following:

1. Social workers must treat clients as "subjects" not "objects."
2. Students must learn some history of social work for context.
3. Education and training not enough—people need experience.

After Vosket left, I met Hermina. She graduated from YSU social work department this past year and is currently doing her master's degree. Without HL present, and in the context of professional practice and expectations, Hermina provided an interesting counterpoint to the students and graduate interviewees in Vanadzor. She was willing to speak more freely than others were, and stated the following:

1. There is a "big difference" between the education she received in social work and practice realities. That is, her education was theoretical and did not prepare her for work with children and families at MSF. She reported having many difficulties connecting theory and practice in a way that helped her organize her work with clients.
2. The most significant gap in her education concerned her ability to work in teams and to respect and understand the diversity of professional expression and experience that is generated through teamwork. She stated that her professors and the curriculum focused only on individual work and on working as an individual with clients. This focus has not been her practice reality.
3. She claims that since most of the professors are/were psychologists, and psychology is the only model they have for teaching, that they placed too much focus on "clinical social work," taking an "individual/clinical" approach in classes that she does not believe reflects the reality for most social workers in Armenia. This approach is not yet applicable in Armenia.

When asked what was missing from her education and what could have made it better, Hermina stated the following:

1. Much more practice experience. She claimed that the supervision at practice sites was "bad," and that these supervisors made students watch and not participate because they did not know how to supervise social workers. She was only allowed to "see, analyze, and observe."
2. They need professors that can speak to classes in terms of case material, specifically related to different cases in the area where they are teaching.

Meeting with MA, Social Worker, at Fund for Armenian Relief—Children's Reception & Orientation Center

MA is a social worker in this street children program and a faculty member at YSU department of social work. Pertaining to social work education and training, MA said the following:

1. The field practicum department needs better supervisors, but she claims they do a good job now. Four faculty members went to UK for experience (a social policy conference), and they now are the supervisors here. She did not explain how a policy conference prepared them to become field instructors.
2. YSU has 20 field placement sites. MA provided a list of sites and a copy of the contract the school makes with sites. She said that nearly all of the sites have qualified supervisors for social workers.

   This contradicts everything I have heard so far, including what HL said.
3. Field placement works like this:
   a. 2nd year—students have one visit to each site for observation and to learn about different services.
   b. 3rd year—students choose placement site and spend four months in intense observation. No client work allowed yet.
   c. 4th year—students return for four-month placement where they get client experience.
4. YSU has written criteria for skills that students must get in practice situations.
5. She said that the department completed a graduate survey that said that students want more practice and practical experience. She thinks that they get a lot of this, and that students just wanted to complain. However, she does think that there could be more interactive/practice courses and that occasionally they need to provide seminars about specific practice situations. MA says she does this now, but there needs to be more of it.
6. She believes that government ministries must compel staff to get at least the certificate level training or they should be fired and replaced by trained social workers. Then, they should have to maintain and improve skills through annual continuing education.

Meeting with DT and KM from World Vision

This turned out to be an excellent meeting, providing concrete information that is usable for this project.

KM is responsible for six inclusive kindergartens, mostly for children with disabilities. However, DT stated that they have begun working with a broader range of children, including those with troubles caused by poverty and other family problems. These kindergartens are in Yerevan and five additional Marz across Armenia.

In each program, they have speech therapists and psychologists. In the Yerevan programs only, they employ social workers. KM stated that they do not employ social workers in the Marz because they are not available. Even here, she stated that the social workers they hire and employ are "weak." (KM is a graduate of the YSU sociology department with some emphasis on social work in 1996.)

KM and DT agreed that social work is the most important part of their programming, but it is also the "weakest link" in their system, primarily because the social workers coming out of school have "no concept" of what a social worker should do. Here are some of the issues:

1. Students are trained theoretically (in psychology) and do not know how to practice as a social worker.

   KM gave an example. A social worker called parents of a child in an orphanage and began the conversation by telling the parents that it is "not right" for them to put their child in an orphanage. This judgment made the parent angry. The parent proceeded to yell at the social worker, who hung up on the parent. Subsequent to this, the social worker approached KM and said that she will "never" call parents again because she was yelled at. KM views this as a classic indication that social work students and graduates do not learn or develop simple, basic skills of client relations (engagement).

2. Students do not learn how to work in teams, so they "try to do everything by themselves."
3. They do not understand how to link clients to other organizations and systems to meet their needs. "They do not understand the referral system."
4. Many of the graduates call themselves "sociologists" instead of social workers. This poses a problem, indeed.
5. They have weak training opportunities.
6. Many see social workers as only "event planners." That is, some believe the only responsibility is to take clients to events. She said that some students and graduates of the program say this about social work, too.
7. In their organization, social workers are doing the following:
   a. activities for children in program
   b. parent training
   c. leading parent support groups
   d. supposed to be completing initial social history along with remainder of team
8. Both claimed that the demand for well-trained social workers would increase, as World Vision begins to undertake a "home visit" program to help deinstitutionalize orphanages, boarding schools, and other long-term institutions. This will be a program of case management and community support, providing linkages to families to needed services and resources.
9. They also need trained social workers in the health sector that includes public health initiatives, especially related to reproductive health and HIV/AIDS.
10. Pertaining to social work training needs, KM and DT said that social workers should be trained in the following areas and ways:
    a. A valid and workable concept of social work.
    b. Need to improve status of social work as a profession.

c. Need more literature translated into Armenian. Some has been translated, but they need more, especially case material.

d. Practical knowledge training. How to engage, assess, plan, and implement plans with clients in the context of a team. KM was especially serious about the need for social workers to know how to gather relevant information, document the information, and "analyze" the information in a professional way to help maximize efforts to help.

e. Need to learn how to collaborate with others. This includes other agencies to share client knowledge about service needs. However, it also includes collaboration between agencies to share training opportunities and experiences, to build the overall social work knowledge, skills, and values in a collaborative way.

f. They need to learn how to deliver services with a longer term, process approach instead of expecting short-term miracles. That is, giving advice doesn't work.

g. The system needs a complete database of referral sources, with specific information on how social workers and clients can access this information. This does not now exist. This is more detailed and relevant than the booklet the NGO Center puts out. This would specifically target social service providers.

h. Need to develop and adhere to a professional code of ethics and standards of training, education, experience, and best practices. This is related to the development of a professional association, either a new one specifically for social workers or the existing section in HL's more global social science organization.

i. Need to establish linkages between professions, for legislative issues and for specific practice issues. Social workers need to learn from, value, and use knowledge and experience from psychologists, and so on, and insist that they be respected as well.

KM has a definite definition of a professional social worker that is completely consistent with the notion of generalist social work and case management, as someone who bridges systems, provides linkages, and provides community support and follow-up to vulnerable clients.

Questions

The information provided in the previous section represents a cross section of information obtained from nearly everyone the author interviewed. Based on this information, please respond to the following questions.

1. Examine the professional literature regarding social work and social work education in former Communist countries. What does this literature say about the issues and problems others faced when trying to establish social work as a respected and functional profession in these countries?

2. Based on the data collected, make a list of the issues, strengths, and barriers regarding social work as a profession in Armenia.

3. Outline a final report that represents that data, issues, and strengths, including recommendations about how to proceed in a way that would be interesting and satisfactory to political leaders and funding sources in Armenia.

4. Write an executive report, complete with recommendations that you would present to the Advisory Committee and USAID that represents your findings and the need/demand for social work in Armenia. Use the following outline to develop your report ideas.

Final Report Outline

I. Methods of Inquiry

II. Issues to Address in Project

1. Assess the current social work training programs that exist in Armenia, including:
   A. Describe types of academic degrees offered.
   B. Vocational programs.
   C. Applicable licensing or certification requirements for practicing social workers.
   D. How do these degrees, programs, licensing, and accreditation elements compare with contemporary western practices?
   E. To the extent possible, how might these issues compare with a realistic standard that might be adopted for Armenia?
   F. Distinguish between caseworkers and qualified social workers.
2. Assess the current opportunity to increase the effective utilization of social workers in Armenia.
   A. Opportunities?
   B. Specific barriers toward such placement?
   C. Identifiable steps to assist in overcoming such opportunities?
   D. Briefly assess the demand for social workers and caseworkers (within context of Armenian environment). Particular emphasis should be on the demand within the Ministry of Social Security, Ministry of Health, regional authorities, and municipalities.
3. Assess the opportunities (in conjunction with PADOO), the opportunities to test new approaches for the application of social work principles and practices in the programs being tested through the new integrated social service centers in Vanadzor and Lori Marz, as well as enhancing other aspects of the social and health pilot programs.
4. Assess capacity of various training and educational programs in Armenia to meet the education and training needs identified in items 2 and 3.

A. Assess current curricula. Are they relevant to the current environment and the demand for social worker training and education?
B. Assess the qualifications and experience of professors, instructors, and trainers.
C. Concentrate on the gaps in the following:
  1. Staffing
  2. Curriculum
  3. Program focus
  4. Outreach
  5. Analyze the "distance education" program at Yerevan State University.
  6. Analyze the role of professional organizations such as the Social Science Association of Armenia in the current status and capacity of social work in Armenia. Identify additional steps that might be taken to enhance these roles.
  7. Recommend short- and long-term human resource capacity building strategies to address needs and demands for social workers in Armenia. The recommendations should:
     a. Emphasize low-cost, practical, and sustainable steps or activities (i.e., distance education) that USAID through the Social Transition Project and the Participant Training Project can initiate immediately to strengthen the social work skills for both academically degreed social workers and caseworkers.
     b. Identify any concerns about the sustainability of training institutions in Armenia that may be used to meet these demands.
     c. Identify possible measures to enhance the sustainability of such institutions.

III. Employ Fields and Practice Settings to Illustrate and Conduct the Needs Assessment

Bibliography _____

Agar, M. H. (1980). *The professional stranger: An informal introduction to ethnography.* San Diego: Academic Press.
DeWalt, K. M., DeWalt, B. R., & Wayland, C. B. (1998). Participant observation. In H. R. Bernard (ed.), *Handbook of methods in cultural anthropology* (pp. 259–300). Walnut Creek, CA: AltaMira Press.
Fellin, P. (1995). *The community and the social worker* (2nd ed.). Itasca, IL: F. E. Peacock.
Johnson, J. L. (2004). *Fundamentals of substance abuse practice.* Pacific Grove, CA: Brooks/Cole.
Johnson, J. L. (1999a). *Crossing borders—Confronting history: Intercultural adjustment in a post-Cold War world.* Lanham, MD: University Press of America.
Johnson, J. L. (1999b). Consulting in Armenia. In L.M. Grobman (ed.), *Days in the lives of social workers: 50 professionals tell the "real-life" stories from social work practice* (2nd ed., pp. 281–288). Harrisburg, PA: White Hat Communications.

Malkasian, M. (1996). *Gha-ra-bagh! The emergence of the national democratic movement in Armenia.* Detroit: Wayne State University Press.

Miller, D. E., & Miller, L. T. (1993). *Survivors: An oral history of the Armenian genocide.* Berkeley, CA: University of California Press.

National Association of Social Workers (2000). *Code of Ethics of the National Association of Social Workers.* Washington, DC: Author.

Rothman, J., & Tropman, J. E. (1995). *Strategies of community intervention* (5th ed.). Itasca, IL: F. E. Peacock.

Shulman, L. (1999). *The skills of helping individuals, families, groups, and communities* (4th ed.). Itasca, IL: F. E. Peacock.

United Nations Development Programme (1993). *Living conditions in Armenia.* Yerevan, Republic of Armenia: UNDP.

Verluise, P. (1989). *Armenia in crisis: The 1988 earthquake.* Detroit: Wayne State University Press.

Wolcott, H. F. (1995). *The art of fieldwork.* Walnut Creek, CA: AltaMira Press.

Zastrow, C. H. (2003). *The practice of social work: Applications of generalist and advanced content* (7th ed.). Pacific Grove, CA: Brooks/Cole.

5

Organizing Social Work in the Republic of Armenia Part II

Jerry L. Johnson

Recap of Part I

The preceding chapter (Chapter 4) presented the foundation and background for my effort to examine the need, demand, and capabilities for professional social work in the Republic of Armenia. Over three weeks in the country, I interviewed stakeholders in the social service and healthcare systems (government and NGO) to collect information pertaining to this project.

In Chapter 4, I presented examples of the information I collected from providers, government ministries, and the Department of Social Work at the State University. This information is representative of the overall wealth of data I collected during my time in the country.

Based on that information, I asked you to answer a series of questions throughout the chapter as if you were the person performing this project. Chapter 4 ended by asking you to write a final report, complete with recommendations, based on the information gathered in the interviews. I provided an outline for this endeavor.

This chapter contains the final report I made to the sponsor and U.S. Mission in the Republic of Armenia. It is repeated in its entirety below.

Final Report
Assessment of Social Work Educational and Training Needs/Capacity in Armenia

Introduction

This is the final report of a three-week Assessment of Social Work Education and Training Capacity contracted through the Academy for Educational Development (AED) in Yerevan, Republic of Armenia. This investigator conducted the assessment in the Republic of Armenia.

According to the terms of reference, the overall purpose of the assessment was to:

1. Evaluate existing social work training capacity in Armenia and any opportunities to reinforce any developments that have taken place thus far.
2. Provide insights as to where demand for trained social workers may be emerging in the social sector, particularly within Government of Armenia (Ministry of Health and Social Security and their affiliated organizations working in local government).
3. Recommend a technical assistance and training program to improve the professional human resource capacity of social workers that would be reasonable within the near and mid-term projections of demand in Armenia.

Methods

The data used to develop the recommendations in this assessment was gathered through a series of meetings with key informants. Special emphasis was given to issues and interests of appropriate government ministries, primarily the Ministry of Social Security (MOSS), Ministry of Health (MOH), and the Ministry of Education (MOE). Using members of the Assessment Advisory Committee (AAC) as a basis for data collection, a snowball sampling method was utilized to identify further individuals and organizations that could provide relevant information for the study. That is, during each interview, respondents were asked to identify other individuals and organizations they believed should be included in the assessment. Contacts and appointment scheduling was completed by AED staffers.

Forty-six (46) separate meetings were held in three weeks. In all, 114 unduplicated respondents were interviewed individually or in groups. The largest group was a class of 30 current students in the distance education program, offered by the Department of Sociology and Social Work at Yerevan State University in Vanadzor. Given the relatively short period for data collection and the number of individuals away on holiday during the period, the range of key informants involved in this study is noteworthy. That is, while claims can be made in any study that important people were excluded, this investigator sought to be as inclusive as possible given time constraints and other factors involved. Below is a comprehensive list of all meetings held during the data collection portion of this needs assessment. Every meeting except one was held in the key informant's office, home, classroom, or place of employment, including several meetings held in Vanadzor. The number in parentheses ( ) indicates more than one meeting and the number.

Government Ministries

1. Ministry of Social Security
   a. Deputy Head of Social Services
   b. Coordinator of Training
   c. Head of Family and Children Department
   d. Deputy Head of Family and Children Department
   e. Head of Department for Disabled Persons
   f. Head of Monitoring and Analysis Department
   g. Local members of Integrated Social Service Center Task Force—Vanadzor
2. Ministry of Health
   a. Head of Health Services
   b. Head of Reproductive Health
3. Ministry of Education
   a. Minister of Education

Social and Health Programs

1. Head—Children's Rehabilitation Center
2. Head—Neurological Hospital #6
3. Head—Narcology Center, Yerevan
4. Head—Boarding School for Visually Impaired, Vanadzor
5. Head—Republican Psychiatric Hospital
6. Head—Elderly House, Nork
7. Head—Stress Centre
8. Head of Psychology/Social Work—Red Cross Rehabilitation Hospital
9. Head—Armenian Relief Fund: Children Orientation Center
10. Director of Treatment—Armenian Relief Fund, Children Orientation Center
11. Social Worker/Faculty Member (YSU)—Armenian Relief Fund.

NGOs

1. Head—Astghik Union
2. Nine members of NGO Union—Vanadzor
3. MSF/France: Street Children Project Team
4. Head—NGO Center
5. Head—UMCOR
6. Head and Project Director—World Vision
7. Head and staff—Mission Armenia
8. Head—Junior Achievement of Armenia

Department of Social Work—Yerevan State University
1. Lyudmila Harutyunyan, Dean of Department of Sociology and Social Work (2)
2. Thirty (30) Distance Education students in classroom—Vanadzor
3. Two graduates of YSU, Masters Degree in Social Work
4. One graduate of Distance Education Program—Vanadzor
5. One faculty member
6. One 1996 graduate of YSU social work/sociology program

Additional Key Informant Meetings
1. Marshall Fischer—USAID
2. Brian Kearney—PADCO, Inc. (2)
3. Social Work Need Assessment Advisory Team
4. Evaluation Team—Social Transition Project (3)
5. Twenty-five FPBP recipients
6. Ten senior citizens, service recipients
7. Ten FPBP recipients in group meeting

Findings

This report follows the outline provided in the terms of reference for this project. All of the findings reported below were derived directly from respondent information and feedback.

1. Assess the current social work training programs that exist in Armenia.
   A. Describe types of academic degrees offered. The Department of Sociology at Yerevan State University offers the only social work degree available in Armenia. This department offers a range of education and training:
      1. Certificate Program. Presently, Yerevan State University (YSU) offers the certificate program through the "distance education" program. Students in these programs complete six-module training in foundation social work theory and methods. Successful completion of this program results in a certificate of completion presented by YSU. Credits earned in the certificate program qualify as credit toward a bachelor's degree in sociology with social work specialty at YSU.
      2. Baccalaureate Degree in Sociology, with social work specialty. YSU offers a four-year baccalaureate degree in sociology with a social work specialty at the University in Yerevan. Students completing this degree have two years of full-time study in social work theory and methods, as well as three field experiences (two for observation in social agencies, one direct field practice with supervision). Presently, this program has graduated 140 students.
      3. Master's Degree in Sociology, with social work specialty. Recently, YSU began offering a master's degree in sociology with a social work spe-

cialty. This is a two-year course of study with field experience, leading to diploma research (thesis). Presently, four (4) students have graduated from YSU with this master's degree.

B. **Vocational programs.** While there are no formal vocational programs in social work in Armenia, YSU faculty has developed training packages for staff of local NGOs and programs. Moreover, Mission Armenia has also developed a series of training topics for local professionals. Presently, all local social work training is under the umbrella of the Department of Sociology at YSU.

C. **Applicable licensing or certification requirements for practicing social workers.** There are no licensing or credentialing standards for social workers in Armenia. As the field and profession are new, these standards have not been developed. Currently, there is a subgroup of the Association for Social Sciences that began discussing and developing education, training, and ethical standards for the profession. However, according to key informants, this process has stalled due to lack of funding.

Licensing and/or credentialing standards for social workers should be a long-term goal of professionals in the field and social work educators. The most productive solution to this issue would be to develop a working professional association of social workers in Armenia to develop education and training standards, credentialing standards, and a mechanism for adopting and enforcing adherence to an acceptable code of professional ethics, as well as best practice standards. This is most effectively done as a function of the social work profession, and not as a mechanism of government.

D. **How do these degrees, programs, licensing, and accreditation elements compare with contemporary Western practices?** These degrees and programs are evaluated more fully below. However, on its face, the programs are equivalent to education and training programs offered in Western countries. In terms of courses offered, topics, and level of expected field practicum experiences required, all three programs offer content consistent with accredited schools of social work in the West. However, as discussed below, the lack of experienced social work practitioners for teaching and field practice supervision represents a significant gap in services. That is, without trained and field-experienced social workers for teaching and supervision, the level of competence falls below contemporary Western social work standards.

E. **To the extent possible, how might these issues compare with a realistic standard that might be adopted for Armenia?** Despite the comments above, this investigator is impressed with the level of achievement in the area of social work training and education, given the relative newness of the curriculum in specific and profession in general. Having been part of the development of social work education in other developing countries, the lack of professional field experience and supervisors is to be expected at this point in the profession's development.

As such, faculty at YSU and other specific NGOs in Armenia have begun developing a realistic set of standards and practices for social work training, education, and practice methods in Armenia. Yet, while these efforts have begun, they are being done in relative isolation. That is, there is no mechanism or incentive for organizations to cooperate. Therefore, NGOs such as Mission Armenia and MSF, along with the Stress Centre, are working toward professional practice standards alone. Barriers presented by a lack of cooperation are discussed under "Recommendations," below.

It would be unrealistic to compare the present programs to Western standards. The issue here is for leaders in the profession, perhaps with guidance from outside experts, to continue developing training, education, and practice standards that are realistic and culturally consistent in Armenia. According to all the data collected in this study, this process is underway. However, without significant and timely assistance, it is questionable whether this progress is sustainable. These issues are considered more fully in the remainder of this report.

F. **Distinguish between caseworkers and qualified social workers.** Below are definitions of the categories of social workers. Please note that the development of a system with an adequate number of qualified social workers takes years. The lack of professionals with this level of education, training, and experience presents a significant barrier presently in Armenia. That is, there are not enough qualified social workers available to supervise and/or teach direct practice social work skills. Hence, we are looking, at least in the beginning, at retraining existing workers while developing supervision and training mechanisms to build and sustain the infrastructure for professional social work in Armenia.

A distinction is made between different social work roles. While these definitions are admittedly "Western" in nature, they fit with the roles most respondents believe are appropriate for social work in Armenia.

1. **Qualified Social Worker:** This definition suggests a more experienced clinical role. Hence, one becomes a "qualified social worker" after higher education (post-graduate degree in social work) and at least 2 years post-graduate clinical experience under the direct supervision of a social work supervisor with a higher level of practice experience. This is a generally accepted standard in the West where the social work profession is mature. It is also the base level of education, experience, and level of supervision required for licensure or certification as a "qualified social worker."

   Qualified social workers serve in multiple capacities throughout the human service system. They can serve as generalist case managers (see below), or as primary psychotherapists, supervisors, directors, and policymakers. They have advanced multidisciplinary knowledge and a high level of practical experience converting theory to practice in direct service contexts. Qualified social workers can work under supervision, but most often are qualified to work independently, or in cooperation with psychiatrists, psychologists, and doctors.

There are many significant barriers to overcome in Armenia before this level of social worker becomes prominent and abundant. By definition, for there to be qualified social workers in a particular system, there must be other "more" qualified social workers in the system to provide supervision and training in field practicum during school, and in a professional capacity in post-graduate employment. There does not appear to be more than a handful of social workers that meet this standard currently practicing in Armenia.

In countries where social work is a new or "young" profession, such as Armenia, one longer-term goal is to develop the foundation that ultimately leads to the development of qualified-level social workers within the field. Presently, the necessary infrastructure barely exists in Armenia. If successfully supported in appropriate ways with a view toward long-term development and capacity building, these professionals can and will emerge in Armenia. It will take time, consistency of vision, and resources, both human and financial.

2. **Caseworker/Case Manager:** This classification is the foundation-level social worker that can emerge over the near and mid term in Armenia. In fact, the foundation for this level social worker is already in place at YSU in its degree and distance education programs, and in other programs (primarily, Mission Armenia) in Armenia.

While many believe that caseworkers and/or case managers receive a general education in social work, they do (and, to be effective, must) attain field-specific knowledge (i.e., disabled children, family dynamics, or the elderly). Additionally, caseworkers and/or case managers are trained to understand that individual and family problems are the result of multiple factors in the social environment and, solutions to these problems are found in exercising resources at these different systemic levels.

Therefore, after assessing client needs as part of a multidisciplinary team, caseworkers/case managers seek creative solutions to client problems by helping clients access and attain the resources they need through referral, advocacy, and direct problem-solving methods. In the west, caseworkers/case managers are the "frontline" social workers that the system of care depends on a daily basis. This is the level of professional that is the critical infrastructure of the social work profession.

2. Assess the current demand for social workers and caseworkers (within context of Armenian environment). Particular emphasis should be on the demand within the Ministry of Social Security, Ministry of Health, regional authorities, and municipalities.

This section of the terms of reference also called for a discussion of specific barriers and steps to overcome these barriers in the Armenian environment. To reduce duplication, these issues are discussed more fully at the end of this report. Here, the primary focus in on the demand for social workers in the Armenian environment, particularly within the appropriate government ministries mentioned above.

For the purposes of this report, "demand" is defined as "recognized need." That is, the criteria used to assess demand for social workers in the various systems and practice areas was one based on the key informant's realization that professional social work services would be an integral and important part of efforts to provide services to specific vulnerable populations in Armenia.

3. Data gathered from interviews and document reviews demonstrated significant demand for social work services in the following areas:

A. **Disabled children and their families.** Consistently, professionals in this field discussed the need to provide comprehensive social work services targeted at improving the treatment and living conditions of disabled children and the family and social support systems of these children. Primarily, this demand falls into the general category of deinstitutionalization of children currently living in boarding schools, orphanages, and hospitals. There are at least two reports suggesting that in addition to the 10,000 children currently living in these institutions, there are another 1,200 to 1,500 disabled children isolated in their homes that do not receive even the most basic of social services and support. Presently, there are some sporadic efforts to provide community-based care for disabled children. However, these services are isolated and minimal.

B. **Family and child dysfunction caused by poverty and other conditions in Armenia.** With the many social and economic changes in Armenia in the last decade, many families are unable to care for their children because of poverty and other social conditions that serve to impair family unity and togetherness. As a result, many children are placed in orphanages and boarding schools because families feel they are unable to economically support their children, choosing instead to turn over responsibility to institutions.

Another subgroup of children in this category has turned to the streets (i.e., selling goods, begging, etc.) as a way of providing additional income to their families. MSF, one NGO currently working with these children, calls these children, "Children in the streets." That is, these children are working the streets to provide income to their families, with the support and encouragement of their families. These conditions have led to the beginning of significant familial breakdowns, child abandonment, and prostitution.

In this area, new developments in foster care, along with the need to provide competent community-based support and referral service to children and families in need represents a significant area of demand for specially trained social workers. As children are removed from institutions or removed from the streets, families and other caregivers need the support and services of trained social workers adept at providing a social assessment and linking these families to the organizations, institutions, and other professionals needed to ease family reunification and provide a chance for long-term family stability.

C. **Services for the Elderly.** Respondents reported a growing demand for social work services with the elderly. As the number of single elderly grows, in conjunction with the extended family's inability to care for elderly family members because of poverty, the number of elderly citizens placed in Elderly Homes has increased dramatically. Moreover, there are also a growing number of elderly citizens living alone, without the support needed to ensure the provision of basic needs, including food, clothing, and health care.

Demand was recognized within MOSS for trained pension workers and caseworkers to provide in-home services to the elderly, as well as in the NGO sector. These professionals recognized the benefit (socially and financially) of the ability to appropriately maintain elderly citizens in their home communities over placing them in homes prematurely. Employees and leaders of Elderly Homes also recognized demand, where the need for family reunification services, along with basic daily living assistance was reported to be a significant need.

D. **Deinstitutionalization (Adults and Children) and Community-Based Care.** This area of demand is specifically related to areas A through C above and more generally related to the system of care in Armenia. The Armenian health and social service system is based on institutions. That is, the primary mechanism for treating people with a wide range of issues is to institutionalize these individuals, often for many years. According to key informants, there is no mechanism in the system to provide for outpatient or community-based care. Most of the individuals interviewed recognized the benefits of community-based care, especially the benefits to their client's overall health and welfare, as well as the financial benefits to the system.

At least three hospital directors have developed systems of triage, where the most chronic and severe patients would receive inpatient care while the rest would be managed on an outpatient basis, including in-home care. Despite these plans, the current system does not provide funding for outpatient care, meaning that funds would have to be redirected from inpatient to community care if these services were to occur. For any system of outpatient or community-based care to develop, a cadre of trained social workers is needed.

E. **Provision of Government Benefits and Services to Vulnerable Populations.** There is significant demand to retrain existing workers in MOSS and MOH who have primary responsibility for meeting the public on a daily basis. Leaders in these ministries recognized the problems in the current system, primarily caused by untrained workers. This represents approximately 700 different classifications of frontline workers in MOSS and MOH.

F. **Other areas of demand.** In addition to the significant demand demonstrated in A through E, the following areas also demonstrated demand for professional social work services. While this demand is present, it is not as significant as areas A through E above.

1. **Refugee services.** This demand was most felt in NGOs outside Yerevan. The NGO Union in Vanadzor reported survey results that placed services to refugees as the most significant area of need in Lori Marz.
2. **Ministry of Justice.** According to at least three respondents, the Ministry of Justice has expressed a willingness to place trained social workers in the prison system of Armenia. In fact, the Ministry has approved social work student placement in the prisons as a field education site.

4. Assess the qualifications and experience of professors, instructors, and trainers.
   A. The observed strengths of this program are as follows:
      1. Development of six training modules—written in Armenian language— that is easily delivered in satellite campuses, by trained teachers and train- ers. This suggests that faculty is developing a model of social work that is tailored specifically to Armenia culture and current social and economic conditions.
      2. Feedback from current and former students suggests that the level of edu- cation and commitment of faculty is excellent. These students reported, and demonstrated in a focus group, retention of the presented social work content.
      3. This format would allow, as technology advances permit, the delivery of case materials and substantive teaching and learning via the Internet and/or CD-ROM technology in the future.
   B. The observed weaknesses of this program are as follows:
      1. Feedback from current and former students suggests that the course mate- rials are "too theoretical" in nature. That is, while students learn the foun- dations of social work, the curriculum does not focus students on developing specific social work skills that can be used in practice.
      2. As would be expected in a country where the social work profession is new, the lack of accumulated case experience by faculty, as well as the lack of case materials for study, is an issue to address if social work education and training is to prove useful to students and participants in their profes- sional responsibilities.
      3. Per interviews with students and faculty, course content in social work is general in nature. Faculty should develop content that provides knowledge and skills pertaining to specific vulnerable populations. This content and focus should be available to groups of students who work with specific populations. For example, students who work with disabled children should have specific course content about this population, tailoring both information and skill development to a specific population that is most rel- evant to the students.
      4. The university should look outside its current faculty to locate experienced practitioners who could provide practical, case-specific content. There are experienced social workers outside the university system that could pro- vide these practice elements to the curriculum.

Recommendations for Action

The following recommendations were developed collaboratively with key informants interviewed during the assessment. Additionally, this investigator presented a
draft report to the AAC during a meeting on August 7 and key members of USAID.
Feedback and input from these meetings are also included in the final recommendations contained below.

Item 7 in the terms or reference requested that both short- and long-term
human resource capacity building strategies to address needs and demands for
social workers in Armenia be recommended. Hence, the recommendations below
are subdivided into three sections:

1. Recommendation 1: Short- to mid-term training and education recommendations.
2. Recommendation 2: Recommendations to enhance the social and health service delivery in Armenia.
3. Recommendation 3: Long-term recommendations to sustain the social work
   profession in Armenia.

Recommendation 1: To develop a foundation of trained generalist social workers by investing in the retraining of existing workers and strengthening social work education at the university level.

The unitary vision of key informants was the need to develop a core of well-trained
generalist social workers across the social service and healthcare systems in
Armenia. To accomplish this, the initial focus should be on retraining existing workers in various systems to arm them with basic and fundamental social work knowledge, values, and skills. Retraining should emphasize social work skills of client
engagement (relationship building), assessment, triage, referral, and follow-up.
Additional skills must include working as part of interdisciplinary teams, basic case
recording skills, and conflict management and resolution.

In a complex and ever changing Armenia, people must negotiate many different systems while encountering a number of social problems, organizations, and
social systems in the course of their daily life. Therefore, to survive and even thrive,
people must cope with crises when they arise. Moreover, people must also learn to
cope and navigate through a social environment that is changing, transforming, and
sometimes environmentally hostile, as well as government and social systems that
change rapidly.

To help vulnerable people in this struggle, it is assumed that social work practitioners, with systems and strength perspectives, understanding of social problems,
problem-solving techniques, social systems, laws, policies, and helping resources
available, and an understanding of the diverse needs is best prepared to work in a
rapidly changing society. Therefore, the social worker, prepared with the necessary
social work knowledge, values, and skills is able to recognize that the target for

intervention may not only be the individual or family, but one or more of the social systems affecting the individual or family such as organizations, social and government institutions, communities, and various social and healthcare institutions in the client's social environment.

To provide students and trainees with a professional foundation, faculty, teachers, and trainers must utilize examples from practice to highlight and underscore social work practice theory and methods, as well as technical definitions of systems in order that students may develop a clear understanding of generalist social work practice.

Education and Training Goals

Those who have completed a program of study in generalist social work practice should be

1. Prepared for entry into the profession as generalist social worker practitioners.
2. Prepared to demonstrate basic understanding of the common human needs of people, especially in vulnerable populations and the communities where they live.
3. Able to identify social problems affecting persons and their environments and how these problems influence individuals, families, small groups, organizations, and communities.
4. Able to demonstrate increasing progress in the development of self-assessment, the professional self and competent practice sensitive to cultural, economic, and social issues in society.
5. Committed to social change in pursuit of social and economic justice, and human rights for their clients and families.
6. Able to use their social work knowledge, values, and skills to enhance the quality and delivery of social services to the individual, family, small group, organizations, and communities where their clients live.
7. Willing to continue learning and progressing in their social work knowledge, values, and skills to improve practice outcomes and, by definition, the lives of the vulnerable populations they work with on a daily basis.

This discussion of training and training/education goals leads directly to the first category of recommendations below.

Recommendation 1A: Systematically retrain Family Poverty Benefit Inspectors and other employees with the various Armenian Government Ministries with basic social work knowledge, values, and skills.

According to some estimates, nearly 700 employees in the different government ministries (Social Security, Health, Justice, and Education) and affiliated programs are called "social workers." However, these individuals lack formal social work education or training. These are the workers on the "front lines" of the current reform initiatives and are the point of interface between vulnerable populations in Armenia and their government. It is important that these contacts be managed in a professional manner.

To accomplish this goal, all ministry employees whose primary job function is to serve vulnerable publics should be compelled to complete the following retraining program:

a. Primary social work training would occur during two 2-week training sessions held 6 months apart for one year. Training would commence in groups of 30 participants.

b. During the primary training period, between 2-week sessions, trainers with case experience will convene 1-day case reviews with training participants each month. Each participant would be required to prepare a case example to be discussed and analyzed by the trainers and other participants designed to provide specific case material and hands-on problem-solving methods to be used immediately in their work with clients.

To begin building long-term training resources, the case materials used during the training could be modified to ensure client confidentiality, and compiled into "Casebooks" for use in future training and in social work courses at Yerevan State University. This training schedule would provide much needed immediate training and a way to begin building a store of local case material for training and teaching in the future. This material would also begin the long process of building a sustainable, truly Armenian social work profession.

c. At the conclusion of the 1-year training process, participants would be given an evaluation examination, comprised of both knowledge items and case vignettes, to measure learning and skill development attained during the training process. Participants not able to attain a passing score on this examination would be required to retake the training to improve skills and knowledge.

d. Successful graduates of this training program would then be candidates to help train and assist future trainees on-site, helping to develop a culture of social work and appropriate social work methods that is sustainable.

Hence, it is recommended that retraining of existing employees be the primary goal of immediate funding and support.

Recommendation 1B: Support the strengthening and expansion of the "Distance Education" program offered by Yerevan State University as a primary vehicle for delivering social work training to ministry workers across Armenia.

While the "Distance Education" program does not fit the traditional Western definition of distance education (i.e., delivery of services via technology), its conception as a series of "satellite campuses" is an efficient and appropriate vehicle for delivering social work training to regions outside Yerevan, given the current lack of state-of-the-art distance education technology (i.e., interactive television). Given that the social work department is located in Yerevan and the demand for social work services encompasses all regions of Armenia, the need to deliver social work training and education outside Yerevan is paramount. As such, the current distance education program has the potential to deliver these services throughout Armenia in a comprehensive and efficient manner. It is recommended that financial support be provided to YSU to further develop, refine, and expand the distance education program in Armenia for the purposes of training social workers.

Recommendation 1C: Support the development of other sources of social work training in Armenia outside (or, inside) Yerevan State University.

It is important to make a distinction between "training" in social work, and social work "education." Social work education, the responsibility of colleges and universities, consists of a series of well-planned and coordinated courses and experiences aimed at providing students with a comprehensive foundation in social work knowledge, values, and skills. By design, social work education is delivered in a more general manner. Its goals are to provide students with a well-rounded general exposure to the social work profession.

Alternatively, social work training imparts specific knowledge and related skills, targeted at specific populations and/or procedures confronted by practitioners in daily work experience. For example, training may be targeted at the specific knowledge and skills needed to effectively work with a "lonely elderly person" in her home. Training suggests some level of personal, educational, and/or professional knowledge base upon which the training content will build. Training courses, whether single or multiple days or weeks, targets the unique population it seeks to train, often basing its content on practice skill building and not theory development.

As such, university professors (in any country) are not always the best or most effective professionals to deliver training, as their approach is often general and tends toward the theoretical. Often, local professionals with significant experience in specific areas are better suited to provide social work training. For example, the programs of the NGO Mission Armenia is an excellent example of community-based social work services in Yerevan. This organization has a well-developed understanding of community-based social work, a systematic social work process, excellent record-keeping procedure, and mechanisms for interdisciplinary cooperation that could serve as a model for other social service and healthcare organizations. There are other people serving for years in a community-based social work capacity that are highly qualified, regardless of academic background, to provide social work training.

Therefore, it is recommended that potential sources of local social work training be identified and encouraged to offer training to the social work community. It is further recommended that faculty and leaders at Yerevan State University look to these sources as a potential resource in its training programs, particularly its distance education program. The qualifications for providing population-specific training (i.e., to MOSS Benefit Inspectors) does not require the same level of education and credential as is required to be a member of the university faculty.

Recommendation 1D: Utilize international expertise in social work effectively to promote an "Armenian" body of social work knowledge, values, and skills.

In this period of professional development and development of the social work profession, there is often a need to enhance local education and training with international "experts" in a particular area of interest. However, relying too heavily on foreign experts can lead to a body of social work knowledge that is irrelevant in the context of Armenian social, political, and economic realities. Yet, foreign experts are often the best and only source of needed information. To account for the cultural difficulties often associated with the use of foreign experts, it is recommended that selected foreign experts always be paired with a local practitioner or team of practitioners during any training event. This would allow for vital information from foreign sources to be immediately contextualized to fit with the particular Armenian circumstance.

This arrangement requires that local practitioner(s) be more than traditional interpreters or translators, but full partners in the training dialogue so that information imported from abroad is immediately understandable in the context of Armenian social work practice. Similarly, given the regional differences in conditions and circumstances between Yerevan and other regions, it is also recommended that this same "pairing" arrangement be made for training within Armenia in an effort to localize any social work knowledge to make it useful in its targeted context.

Recommendation 1E: Provide vehicle for intensive training of social work faculty in the social work profession.

There is a need and demand for faculty members and field practicum supervisors (either university or agency-based social workers) to gain intensive field practice experience as professional social workers. Faculty CVs were reviewed as part of this investigation. From this review, it is clear that the Department of Sociology employs many highly trained persons, with excellent academic and research histories. There are also those faculty members that appear to have significant practice experience, including work in private psychology clinics and as sociological researchers. While this experience and level of achievement is noted, as one would expect in a country and university new to the social work profession, most of these distinguished faculty lack professional practice experience in social work.

By definition, social work practice experience is qualitatively different from experience as a psychologist or sociologist. Moreover, acquiring expert-level knowledge of social work theory cannot be substituted for the unpredictability of practice with human beings in need, and does not allow for the integration of theory and practice that the students (and professionals) interviewed during this assessment claimed was needed, but missing.

This is both a long- and short-term issue that needs addressing if social work education and training is to be sustainable in Armenia. The lack of this level of training and knowledge among social work faculty leads to a long-term cycle of education and training that perpetuates a "theoretical" profession, unable to bridge the theory and practice divide.

Therefore, it is recommended that selected faculty from Yerevan State University be allowed to acquire a Master's Degree in Social Work (MSW) abroad. Many universities in the United States, for example, allow visiting faculty from abroad to complete the MSW degree in one full year of study. The degree program is primarily based in field practicum experience, supervision, and training. While expensive, providing the support so that interested university faculty can acquire their MSW degrees will provide the foundation for long-term sustainability of a social work profession in Armenia.

Recommendation 1F: Work creatively to provide appropriate and experienced field practice supervisors for students and trainees to enhance practice knowledge, values, and skills.

Given the universally expressed demand for competent and experienced practice supervision, primarily for social work students involved in field practice experiences, it may be in the best interest of the university to make creative arrangements for on-site supervision in field practicum. For example, in locations that lack social work supervisors, appoint a committee of supervisors from the practice community, affiliated with the university, to be so-called traveling social work supervisors. That is, these practitioners, while not being part of the regular faculty, become affiliated with the department based on practice experience and not academic credentials.

In reviewing the list of practicum sites provided by the university, it appears that the department is using a creative approach to on-site supervisors when it comes to academic background. For example, the listed mentor at MSF is an Armenian social worker who has no formal background in social work, but as a history teacher. The department is to be applauded for being willing to utilize the resources available while not holding to an academic standard that would disallow such creativity.

However, the department is now encouraged to extend this creativity to providing the arrangements and resources for supervisors even if the supervisor does not work in a particular facility. Students placed in these organizations would have an on-site mentor who would team with an affiliated faculty member to provide social work supervision and training. The primary benefit of this arrangement would be to open the university and its students to placement sites that may not be accessible due to the lack of on-site, qualified supervisors.

Therefore, it is recommended that the university be encouraged and supported as necessary to seek out creative mechanisms to provide on-site field practice experience in a wide range of social service organizations, beyond those with existing social work mentors located on-site.

It is also recommended that the university develop more and varied practice sites, beyond the 20 sites listed in the documentation provided to this investigator. During the course of this investigation, many programs were visited that could provide excellent field experiences for students (i.e., Red Cross Rehabilitation Center).

Recommendation 1G: Provide low-cost intensive retraining for staff in social service and health service programs.

The university or other organizations (see Recommendation 1C) should be supported in the effort to develop specific social work skills training packages for delivery to any social service or health organization that wants or needs such skill development. These training packages could be based on some variation of the program explained in Recommendation 1A, or be delivered in a unique manner that fits the needs of a particular agency. During this investigation, it became clear that many programs, after hearing about the value and role of social work in their work, would want on-site training for their staff. These programs, with the capability to specifically tailor the training content to the unique needs of a particular organization, are highly needed.

Presently, the university social work program has the capacity to provide short-term social work training. Responses from professionals in the field who have participated in this training stated clearly and unanimously that the training was interesting, but not specifically tailored to the organization's population and service needs. That is, this training was primarily concerned with teaching general social work history, methods, and theories. As stated earlier, while this information can be valuable as part of a social work educational process, most of the content in training projects must be skill-based and targeted at specific populations.

Therefore, it is recommended that the motivation and resources be provided to encourage the university or other organizations to develop on-site training packages for social service and health organizations that acquire or discover the need for social work training.

Recommendation 1H: Create long-term project to develop cadre of qualified social workers.

The need to develop a base of highly trained social work professionals to become leaders in the profession for the future is critical to the sustainability of social work in Armenia. While this issue was addressed above (see Recommendation 1E), this recommendation is targeted at current practitioners or recent graduates of the university with excellent potential as social work leaders in Armenia.

To accomplish this, it is recommended that training partnerships be developed between the Armenian government and international organizations or governments, whereby the Armenian government funds initial training of new social workers in Armenia. Following this training, international organizations or governments would fund advanced training (perhaps, including acquiring an MSW degree abroad with supervised field experience) to bring the student/trainee's knowledge and skill level to international social work standards.

In exchange for the opportunity to participate in this excellent training experience, these individuals would make a commitment to Armenia that compelled them to work in high-risk sites, or sites where demand is high, for a specified period after completing their training. For example, upon completion of training, these future social work leaders could be placed in a particular program or agency where their expertise is most needed. (i.e., disabled children, etc.).

The advantages of this type of investment in human resource capacity building are numerous, covering the short and long term. These highly trained specialists could become future faculty members, trainers, supervisors, and directors of important social work programs in the future. During the service commitment period, these individuals could serve as on-site supervisors for social work students, and/or provide retraining to workers in social assistance agencies. They would have the capacity to have an impact on future program direction, including involvement in future social legislation and government planning processes. Moreover, this type of program would signal a commitment to long-term capacity building in Armenians as the owners and future of their own social service sector, and in the training of the army of professionals that will be needed to provide services to their citizenry. This type of long-term commitment would help develop a cadre of future leaders of an Armenian social work profession, and stimulate the development of well-trained social workers in the future.

Recommendation 2: Enhancing Service Delivery

Recommendation 2A: Create targeted pilot projects to place social workers (internships and professional).

This recommendation would provide for the placement of social workers (either students or trained professionals) into specific selected sites where need is greatest. For example, a social work practitioner should be placed in the Integrated Social Service Center. In addition to daily casework, this specially trained social worker could also train the Family Poverty Benefits inspectors and staff from the other participating MOSS departments on-site.

Recommendation 2B: Develop funding mechanisms and incentives to create community-based or outpatient treatment and support models to aid in deinstitutionalization, to utilize limited funds in a more efficient manner, and to provide social protections to vulnerable children, families, and adults.

There is no funding in the Armenian system for outpatient or community-based aftercare services. Programs that want to provide this type of care must attempt to pay for these services from funds designated for inpatient treatments. Since government reimbursement for inpatient is unable to pay current expenses, it is nearly impossible for programs to pay for innovations, such as community-based outpatient care. Among the many problems with this funding system, it encourages doctors to institutionalize patients because of the financial incentive, meaning that many institutional beds are filled with patients who do not require inpatient treatment. Hence, a new system that focuses on placing clients in their home communities whenever possible, with the social and health supports provided by specially trained social workers, would lead to significant deinstitutionalization, as well as use scarce funding more efficiently.

     Therefore, USAID should support partnerships to develop community-based care initiatives that allow institutions to deinstitutionalize. To accomplish this goal, a cadre of trained social workers/case managers will be required to perform the community assessment, support, and to provide the necessary linkages for clients to the necessary resources in their home communities.

Recommendation 2C: Support and expand the Integrated Social Service Center idea that is an integral part of the STP program.

The idea of a nationwide system of Integrated Social Service Centers would greatly enhance efficiency in the Ministry of Social Security but also help make the system user-friendly for its clientele. This system will also increase the opportunities to deliver comprehensive social work training to MOSS employees and ultimately enhance the ability of these newly trained social workers to collaborate, leading to a more systemic and comprehensive approach to the delivery of social services through this important government ministry.

Recommendation 2D: Promote opportunities for employment of trained social workers in current social and health programs, including schools, orphanages, rehabilitation hospitals, psychiatric hospitals, and homes for elderly.

While it is not necessarily within the purview of USAID to provide specific funding to programs to cover staff salaries, it would be possible to include in any new

RFP program initiatives where social services are involved language specifying the need to employ trained social workers to deliver these services. In addition, existing programs should be encouraged to hire newly trained social workers or participate in staff retraining to ensure that vulnerable populations receive the best possible treatment and care.

Recommendation 3: Provide support and incentives to stimulate long-term development of the social work profession in Armenia.

Recommendation 3A: Assist to establish a viable Armenian Association of Social Workers.

The existence of a strong and viable association of social workers in Armenia is central to the future establishment and sustainability of the profession. Presently, there is local pressure to include social workers as one arm of the larger Social Science Association. This is not recommended. The lack of visibility a new professional association would have as a subgroup of a larger organization, competing with older, more established professions for attention and visibility may render it useless. Hence, it is recommended that an Armenian Social Workers Association be supported that exists apart from the Social Science Association.

This association can provide public visibility for the profession, as well as become the group that establishes an Armenian system of credentialing, best practices, and a professional code of ethical conduct. Not only do Western countries and many developing countries in Eastern and Central Europe have national social worker associations, but also there is an International Association of Social Workers that promotes the profession worldwide. Therefore, it is recommended that a partnership grant be considered, once a group is in place, to allow it to consult and associate with the International Association of Social Workers and/or social work associations abroad.

Recommendation 3B: Social workers must seek to become an integral part of future legislative and social policy development pertaining to human services in Armenia.

In a related recommendation, professional social workers should be encouraged and supported to become politically active in the development of social welfare legislation and social policy that affects vulnerable populations in Armenia. Furthermore, this action should have a goal of convincing the Armenian government to include language requiring trained social workers in social policy and programs sponsored by the state.

Several developing countries in Eastern and Central Europe have developed social work professions, including involvement in social policy and legislation. To encourage and support this effort, USAID could provide funding for study tours to these countries, or western countries, where interested social workers could learn the macro-level skills needed to influence the legislative and social policy process.

Recommendation 3C: Support and encourage a process for system-wide education about the role of social work, social workers, and how these trained professionals can benefit various social and health service programs.

The newly emerging profession of social work needs to provide education to the human service sectors in Armenia as a primary vehicle for increasing visibility, enhancing professional understanding, and opening positions in the various social programs currently operating in Armenia. While an organized effort at public relations and education would inevitably involve some difficult negotiations between professional disciplines regarding status and power, it is a necessary part of developing an emerging profession. This effort should become part of any newly established social worker association. It is recommended that funding be made available to create a public relations and education initiative that informs doctors, government officials, program directors, and the public about the role and skills social work brings to human service in Armenia.

Opportunities for Action in the Current Environment

1. **Demand for social workers and apparent interest by local leaders.** This assessment discovered that there is significant demand in the system for trained social workers and an avid interest, along with open expressions of support from government and human service sector leadership for this profession's establishment in Armenia.
2. **Apparent interest of foreign governments and international funding sources.** There also appears to be heightened interest from foreign governments and international donors to support policy initiatives and projects to reform how social and health services are delivered in Armenia. Hence, this is an excellent time to offer support in the areas described above.
3. **The skill, commitment, and leadership in SW provided by YSU.** HL and her faculty have done a commendable job of bringing social work education and training to the forefront in Armenia. The idea and implementation of "distance education" is a testimony to the creative spirit of this group. With correct support and encouragement, Armenia has a credible infrastructure upon which to build a social work profession in the future.
4. **A highly educated workforce already serving in "social work" capacities.** Despite a profound lack of social work training and education among those currently serving as "social workers," these individuals are highly educated and trained professionals. That is, they are, for the most part, people who understand the need for professional training and skill and who know how to learn and apply skills in a professional capacity.

5. **The historical ability of Armenian people and systems to adapt, change, and thrive through difficult circumstances.** Throughout history—and in contemporary times—the Armenian people have suffered, adapted, and thrived through more than their "share" of tragedy, violence, and massive systemic changes. Given this history, this country will be quick to adopt any new profession and/or systems—such as social work—that will help promote health and the ability to thrive in their newly emerging and developing country.

Barriers to Action in the Current Environment

1. **Funding and economic situation in Armenia.** Paradoxically, the time that most countries need a social work profession occurs when that country is least able to afford it. This is the circumstance in Armenia today. Hence, it is imperative that foreign organizations demonstrate the foresight and commitment to support the emergence of professional social work through sustainable training, employment, and the professionalization of its members in the short and long term until such time when the profession becomes embedded as part of Armenian human service sector culture.

2. **The problem of cooperation.** The problems of professional cooperation and communication were the single most common issue presented during this investigation. Some said it is a holdover from Soviet times; others blamed the funding cycle that promotes competition over cooperation, while one leader even suggested that the inability to cooperate in Armenia was "genetic." Whatever the reason(s) for this, it became apparent that this is a significant barrier to the development of social work as a viable profession.

   Ironically, social work is a known as a "bridging" profession, in that it is designed and based on the ability to connect organizations and professions together in a cooperative way to serve its clientele. Given the scarcity of resources, the most important issue uncovered in this investigation may be the need to promote and stimulate cross-system cooperation by training new or existing social workers to function across systems, in a cooperative manner. This is consistent with the efforts of USAID and PADCO to create an Integrated Social Service Center in Vanadzor or to have social workers deliver services that overlap between departments in MOSS such as services for the disabled, families, and children, and benefits provision.

   Similarly, can government agencies and NGOs work together with the university toward cooperative training agreements and, perhaps, supervision? Can they work together to provide field practicum agreements and arrangements for students, when this cooperation may involve sharing supervision and experience? In all of these areas, there is a need for public (government) and private (NGO) partnership to stop duplication of services, freeing up vital resources for new and creative human service initiatives.

3. **Remnants of Soviet system.** In addition, the previous system's contribution

to the problem of cooperation discussed above and the belief that laws alone force people to behave in accordance with the law, the human service system's belief in rigidly hierarchical, medically based service provision where nobody challenges the doctor's opinion is a significant barrier to the development of social work in these organizations. In addition, the inclination to institutionalize almost all social and health problems is also a significant holdover from Soviet times. While these beliefs are also common to one degree or another in western countries, these attitudes will have to change if social work and community-based services are to take hold in Armenia.

4. **Lack of professional understanding of social work.** This issue was addressed above in Recommendation 3C.

5. **Short-term relief vs. long-term capacity building mentality.** There are many in this country, both Armenian and foreign professionals, who believe that the funding strategies to date have focused more on short-term relief instead of long-term capacity building. If social work is to become a viable profession in Armenia, integrated throughout a newly reformed human service system, then any funding initiatives will have to be presented with incentives toward long-term capacity building. That is, developing a profession that becomes "of" the host country instead of imposing foreign methods onto a country will help ensure that the social work profession becomes sustainable over the long term.

Summary and Outcome

I left not knowing if anything would come of this project. Within three months, I received a Request for Proposal (RFP) from the sponsor asking for organizations to bid on providing the services recommended in the report. I decided not to bid for the contract. However, 18 months later, I learned that a comprehensive training program was in place, and that all 700 MOSS and MOH social workers had received the first part of the training program. Moreover, Armenian students were exchanged with American students for training and, at least two Armenian social work students will receive their MSW degrees in the United States. I was told that other recommendations were operating, and within a few years they expect the report to be fully implemented.

Questions

1. **How did your draft report compare to the final report submitted by the author?**

2. **Examine the differences, and evaluate your ideas compared with the author's. In your opinion, did the author miss anything significant? If so, please explain.**

3. **Overall, evaluate the project by using your knowledge, the professional literature, and the information provided in the case.**